RECORDED VERSIONS GUITAR

AUTHENTIC TRANSCRIPTIONS
WITH NOTES AND TABLATURE

THE JIMI HENDRIX EXPERIENCE

WINTERLAND

(HIGHLIGHTS)

Music transcriptions by Jeff Jacobson and Paul Pappas

ISBN 978-1-4584-3647-4

EXPERIENCE
HENDRIX™

EXCLUSIVELY DISTRIBUTED BY

HAL•LEONARD®

7777 W. BLUEMOUND RD. P.O. BOX 13819 MILWAUKEE, WI 53213

Visit Hal Leonard Online at
www.halleonard.com

Fire

Words and Music by Jimi Hendrix

Tune down 1/2 step:
(low to high) E♭-A♭-D♭-G♭-B♭-E♭

10/12/68 - 1st show

*Chord symbols reflect implied harmony.

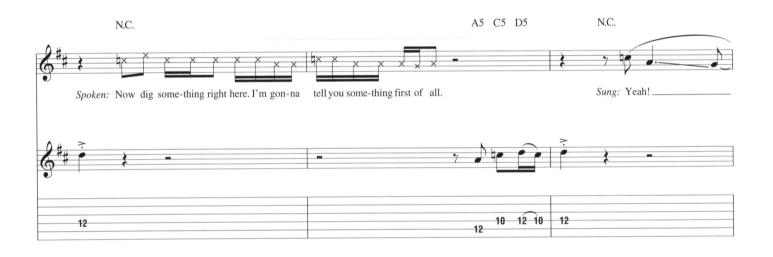

got a new fool, __ ha, I like it like __ that. I have on - ly one

itch - in' de - sire, __ let me stand __ next to your fire.

End Riff A

let ring

Chorus

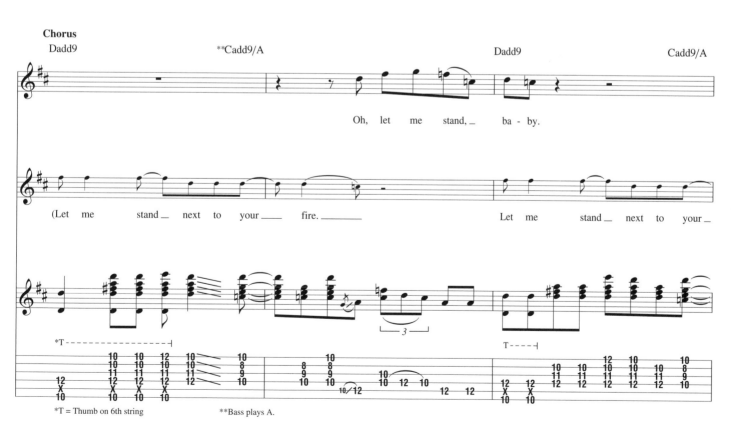

Oh, let me stand, __ ba - by.

(Let me stand __ next to your __ fire. _____ Let me stand __ next to your __

*T = Thumb on 6th string   **Bass plays A.

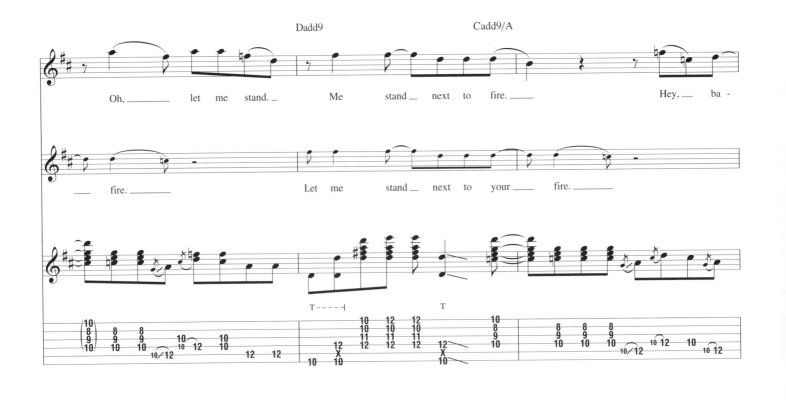

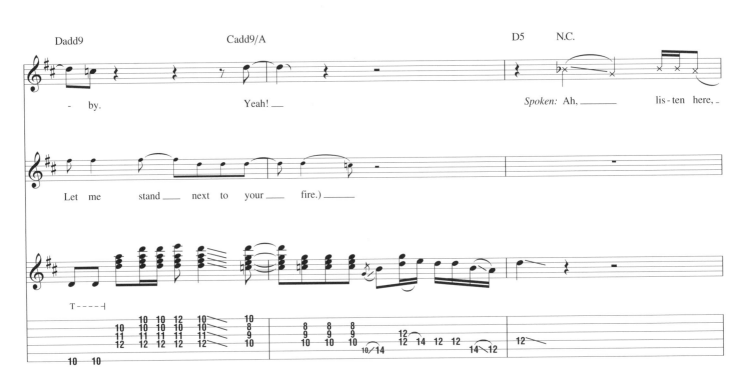

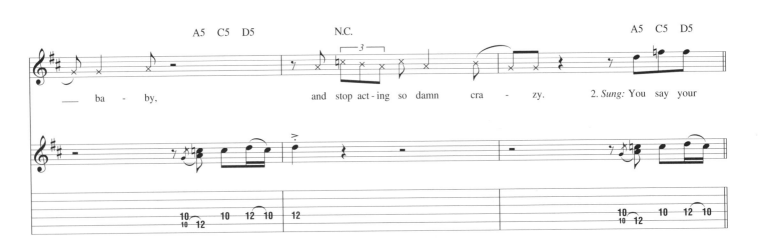

Verse

mom ain't home, _ it ain't my con-cern. Don't play with me _ and you won't get burned.

I have on - ly one itch-in' de-sire, _ *Spoken:* let me stand _ to your...

Chorus

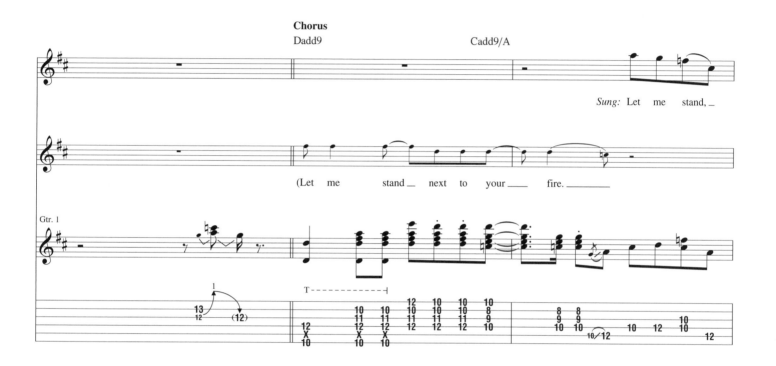

Sung: Let me stand, _

(Let me stand _ next to your _ fire. _)

ba - by. Oh, _ let me _ stand, _ ba - by.

Let me stand _ next to your _ fire. _ Let me stand _ next to your _

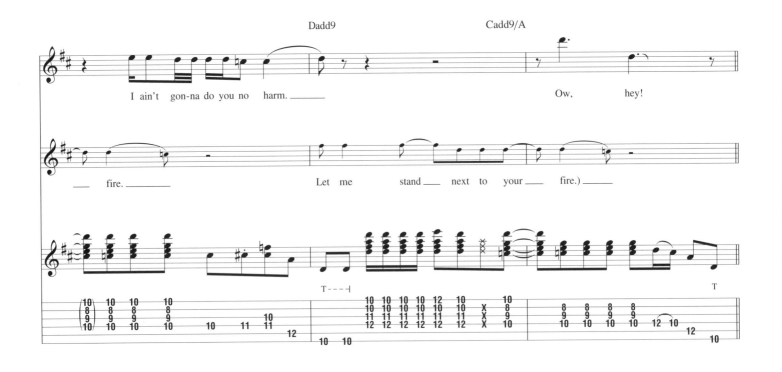

I ain't gon-na do you no harm. _____ Ow, hey!

_____ fire. _____ Let me stand _____ next to your _____ fire.) _____

Bridge

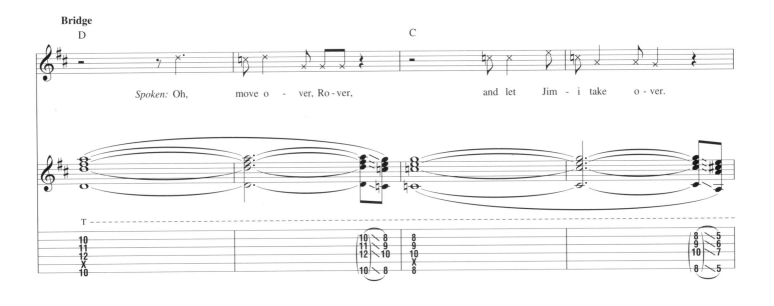

Spoken: Oh, move o - ver, Ro - ver, and let Jim - i take o - ver.

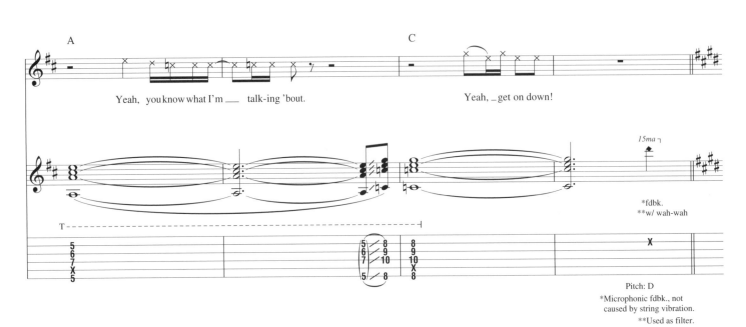

Yeah, you know what I'm ____ talk-ing 'bout. Yeah, ___ get on down!

*fdbk.
**w/ wah-wah

Pitch: D
*Microphonic fdbk., not
caused by string vibration.
**Used as filter.

Guitar Solo

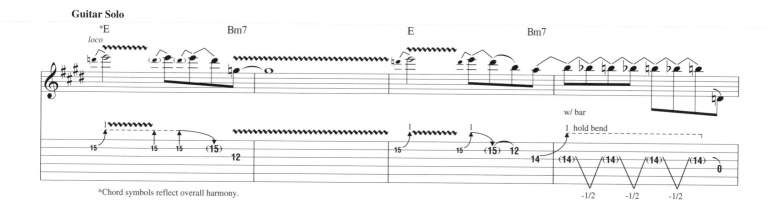

*Chord symbols reflect overall harmony.

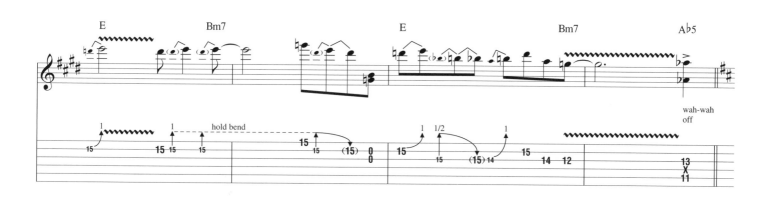

Interlude

Yeah! _____

That's what I'm __ talk-in' 'bout. __

Now dig the drum-mer, now.

Yeah! ___

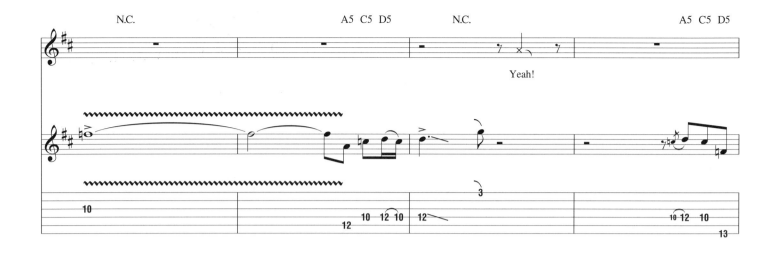

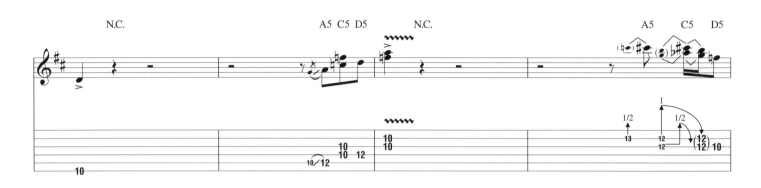

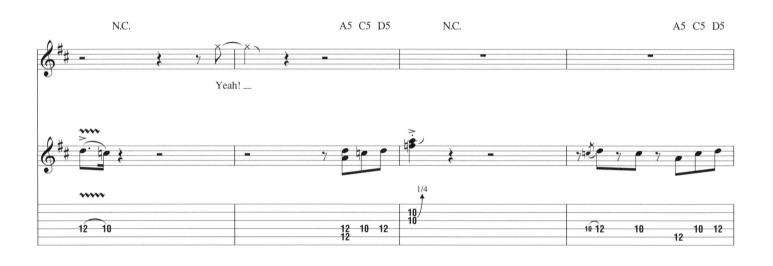

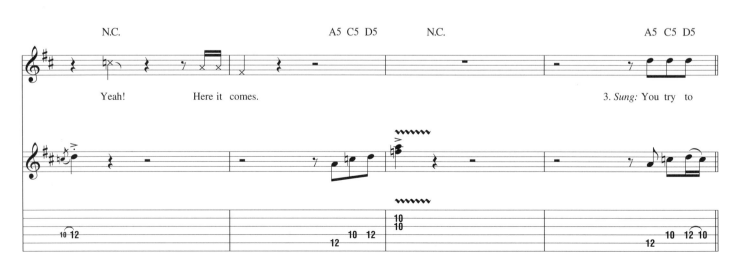

Verse

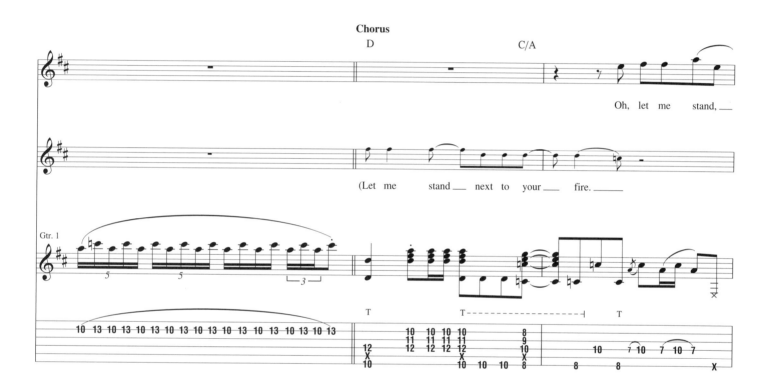

Chorus

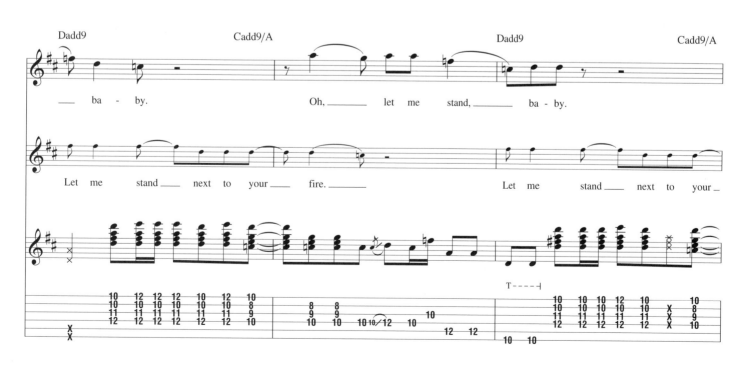

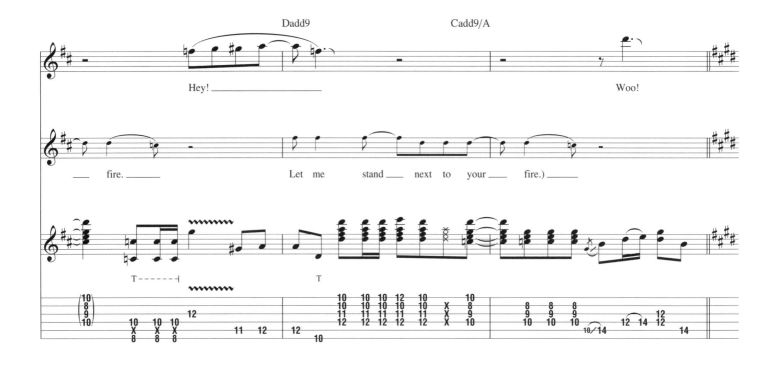

Dadd9   Cadd9/A

Hey! _____ Woo!

__ fire. _____ Let me stand ___ next to your ___ fire.) _____

Guitar Solo

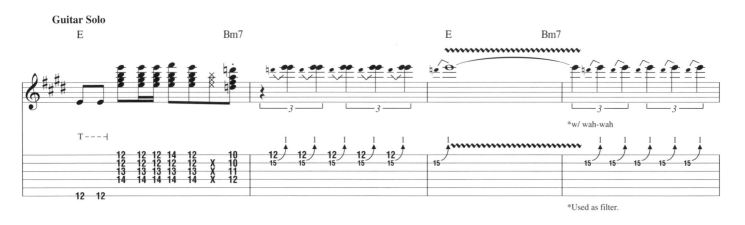

E   Bm7   E   Bm7

*w/ wah-wah

*Used as filter.

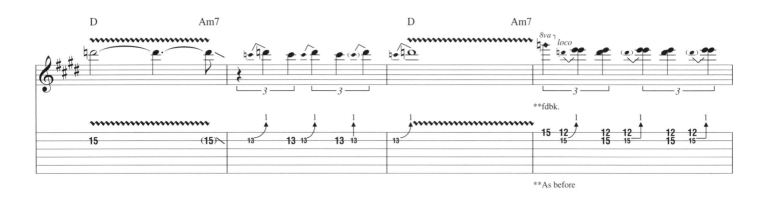

D   Am7   D   Am7

**fdbk.

**As before

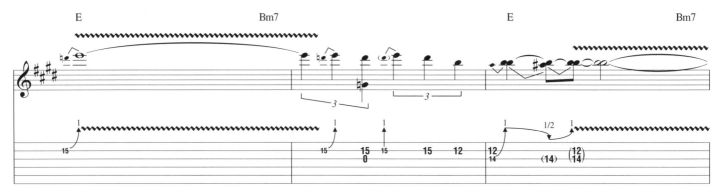

E   Bm7   E   Bm7

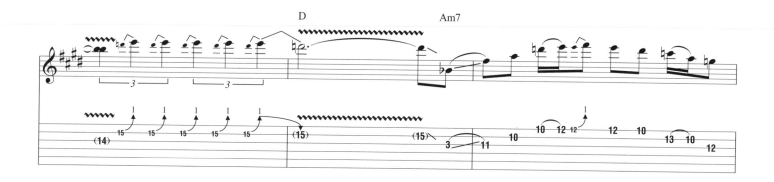

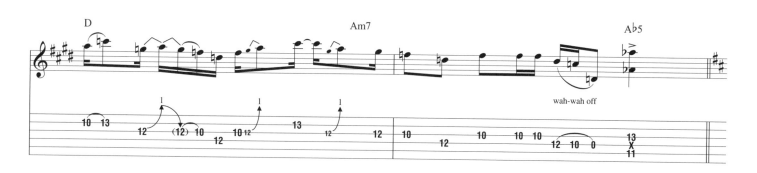

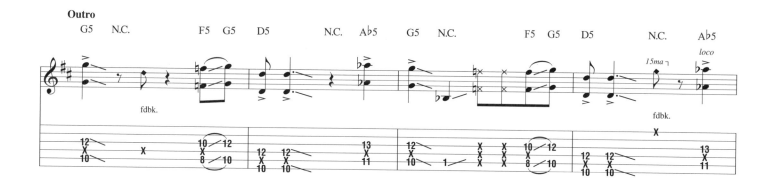

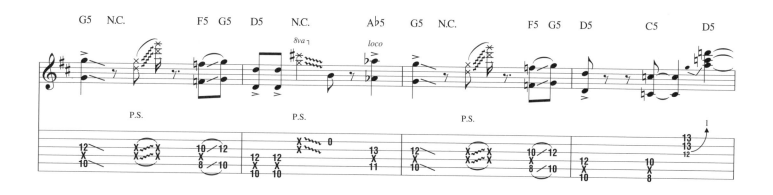

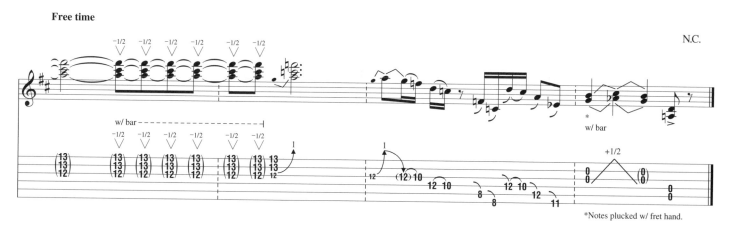

Foxey Lady

Words and Music by Jimi Hendrix

Tune down 1/2 step:
(low to high) Eb-Ab-Db-Gb-Bb-Eb

10/10/68 - 1st show

Intro
Free time

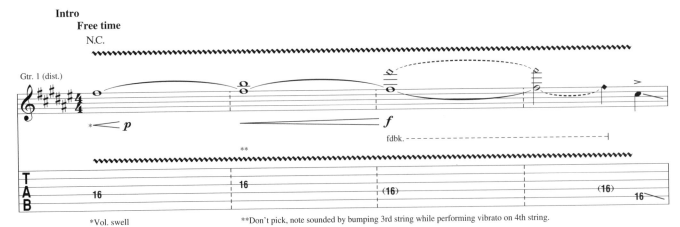

*Vol. swell   **Don't pick, note sounded by bumping 3rd string while performing vibrato on 4th string.

Moderately slow ♩ = 90

***Chord symbols reflect implied harmony.
†T = Thumb on 6th string

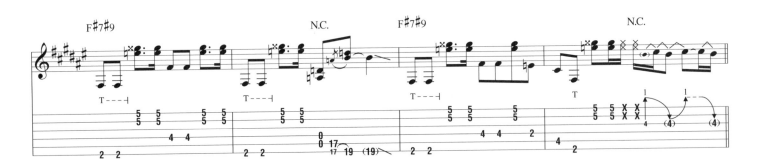

Verse

1. Uh, you know you're a   cute lit-tle heart-break-er. ___   Yeah, ___   fox-ey.

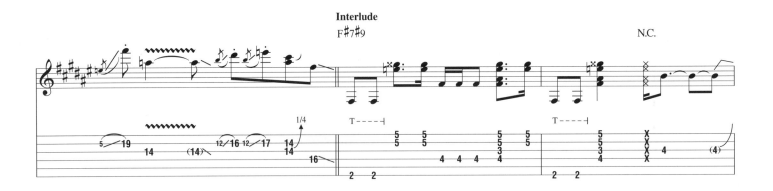

Interlude

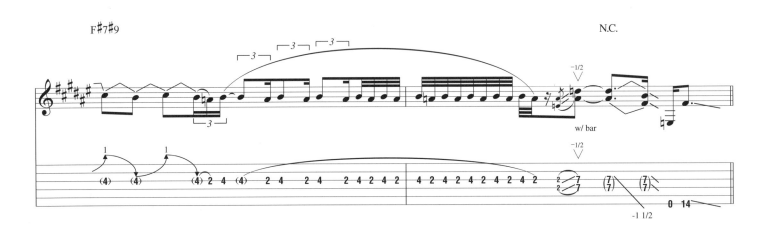

Verse

2. I see you come down on the scene.

Fox-ey.

Make me wan-na get up and scream.

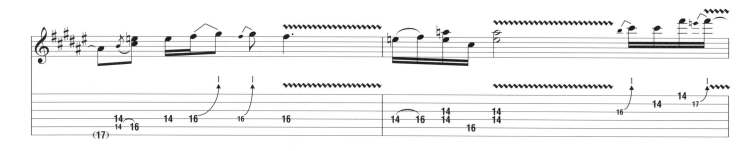

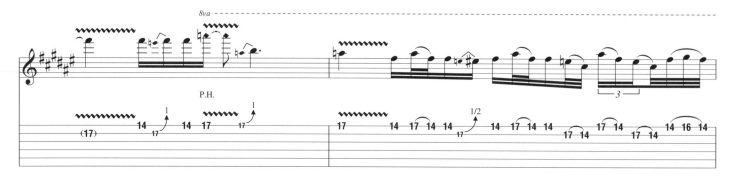

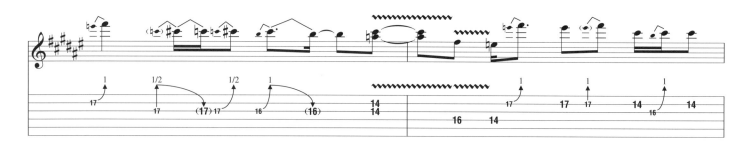

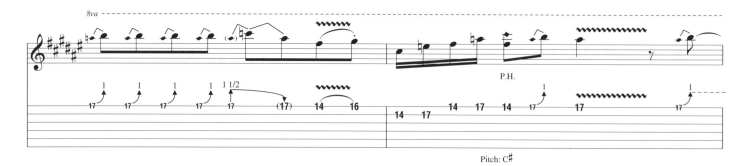

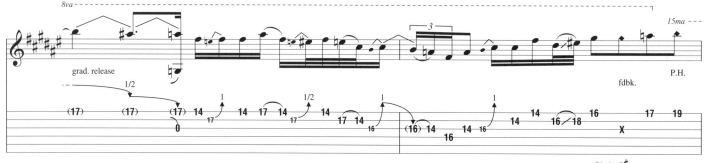

Pitch: G#

*2nd string caught under bend finger.

Pitch: G#

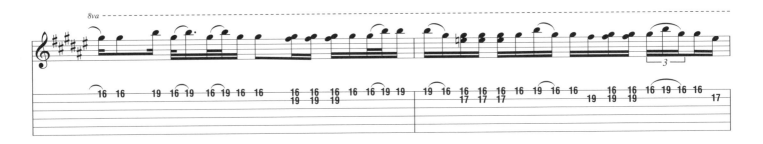

Pitch: C#   D

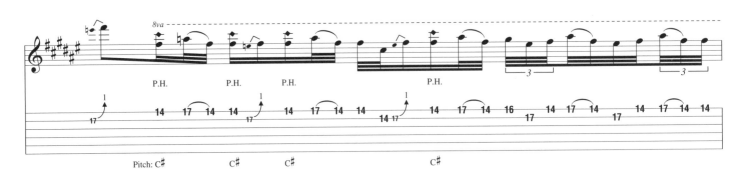

Pitch: C#   C#   C#   C#

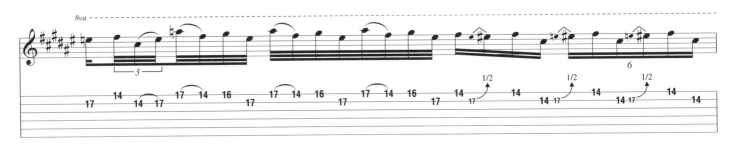

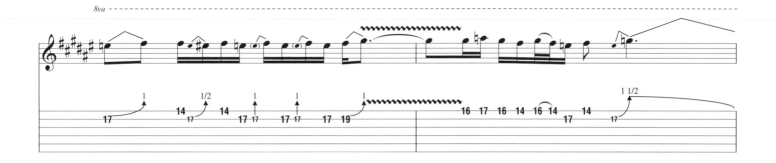

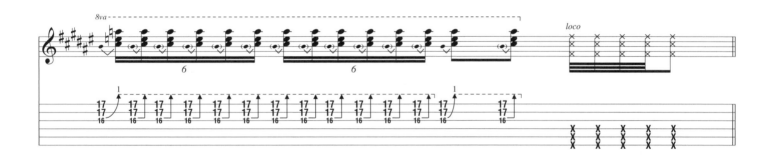

Chorus

I've made up my mind, __

I'm tired of wast-ing all my pre-cious time,

You got to be all, mine.

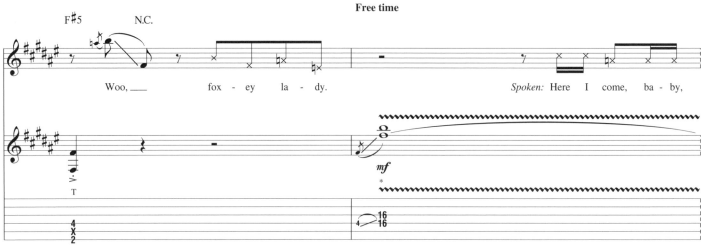

Free time

Woo, ___ fox - ey la - dy.

Spoken: Here I come, ba - by,

*Top note sounded by touching 3rd string while performing vibrato on 4th string.

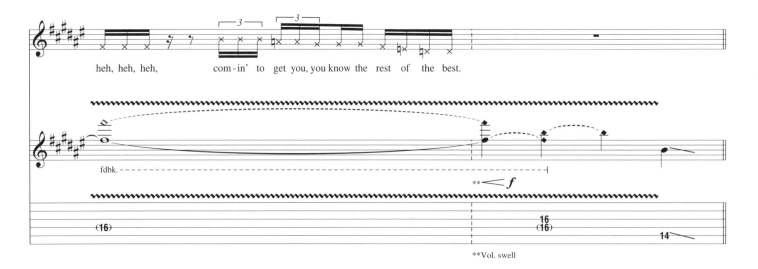

heh, heh, heh, com - in' to get you, you know the rest of the best.

**Vol. swell

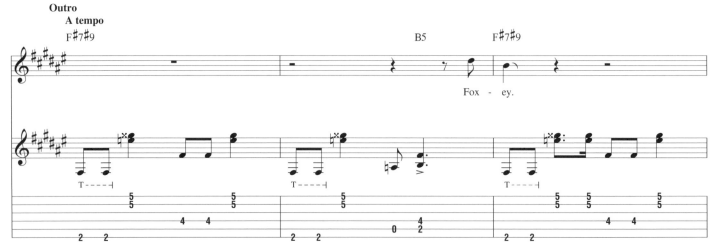

Outro
A tempo

Fox - ey.

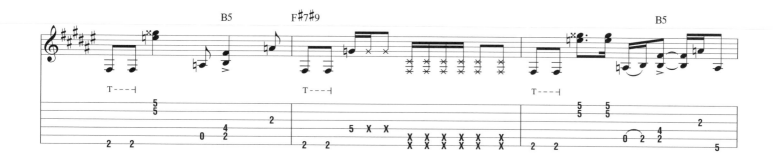

B5   F#7#9   B5

F#7#9   B5

Spoken: You're so good, ba - by.   I'm out   of tune but, hell...

Free time

N.C.

F#7   N.C.

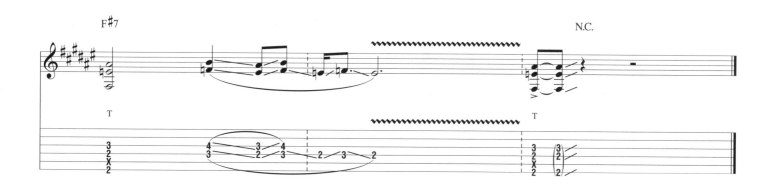

Like a Rolling Stone

Words and Music by Bob Dylan

Tune down 1/2 step:
(low to high) Eb-Ab-Db-Gb-Bb-Eb

10/12/68 - 1st show

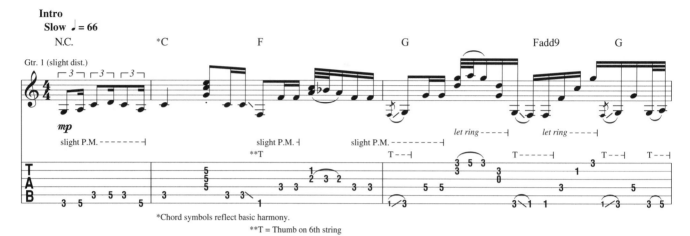

*Chord symbols reflect basic harmony.
**T = Thumb on 6th string

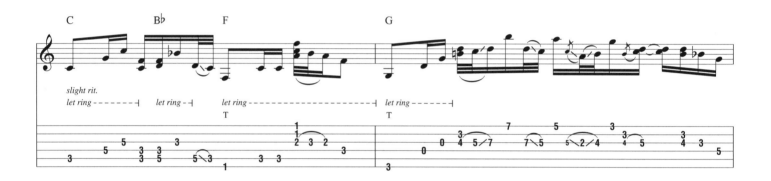

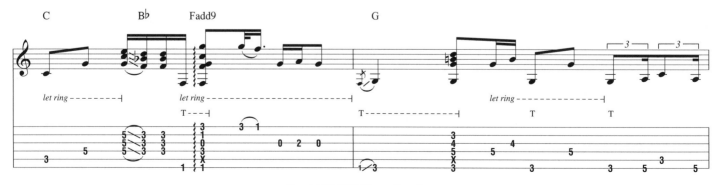

Spoken: Here's a song written by Dylan.

It's a thing called "Like a Rolling Stone."

1. Once up-on a time   you dressed so fine, __   threw the bums a dime __ in your prime,

a, did-n't you?

Peo-ple call, __   say, "Be-ware doll, __   you're bound to fall," __   and you thought they were all __

a, kid-din' you.

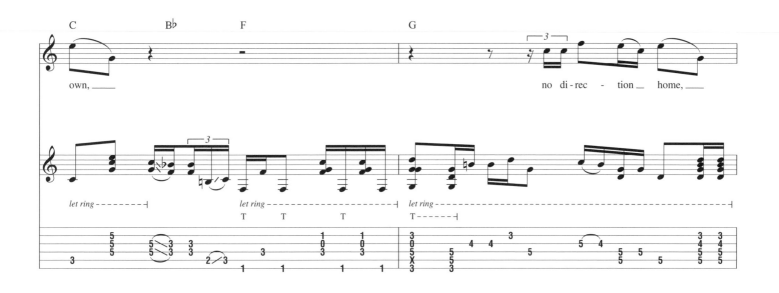

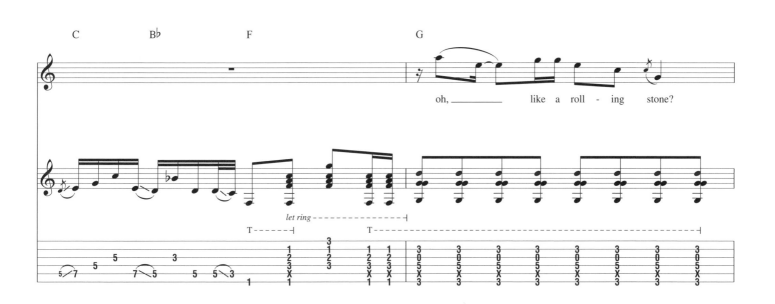

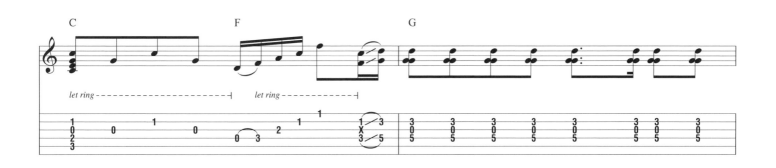

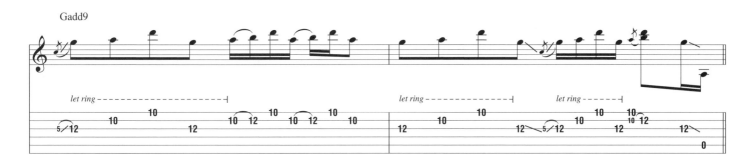

Gadd9

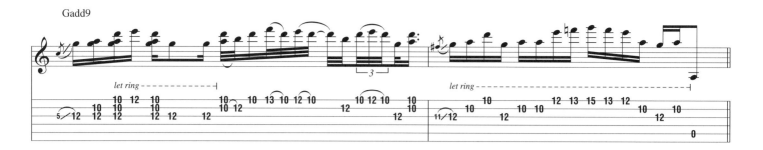

Guitar Solo

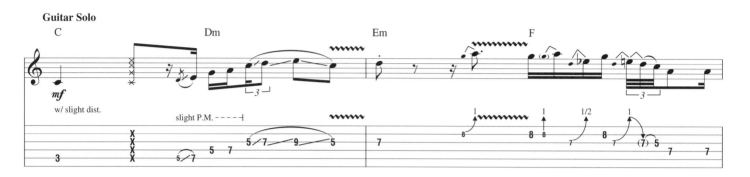

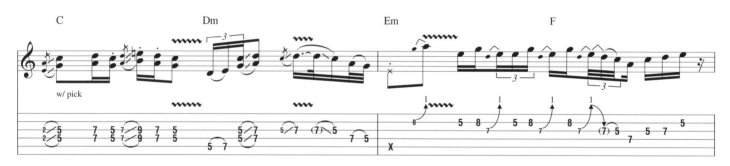

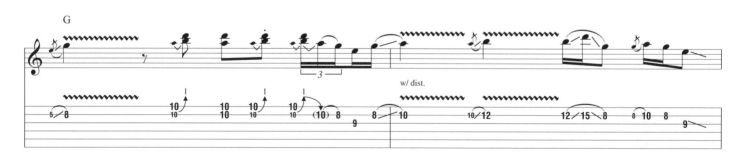

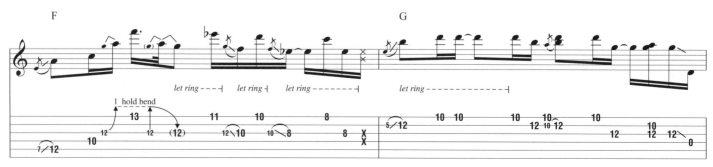

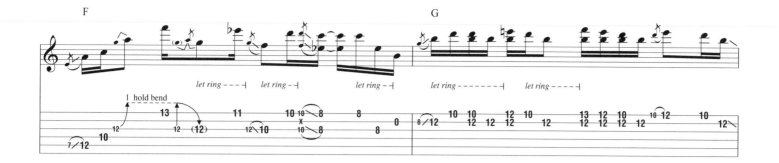

*Used as filter.

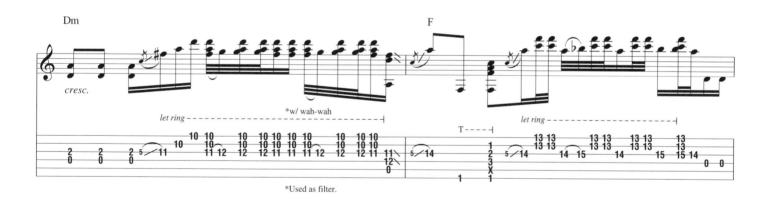

How does it   feel? _

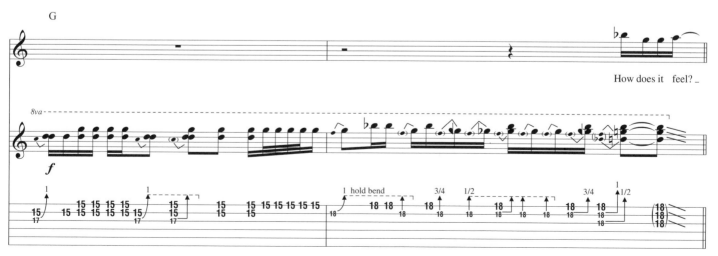

tricks for you,   tricks for you,   ba - by, uh.

You nev - er un - der - stood _ that it ain't no good,   you know good and well you should-n't let oth-er peo-ple get your _

kicks for you.

I see you rid-in' 'round _ town   in a chrome horse   with your _   dip-lo - mat _

38

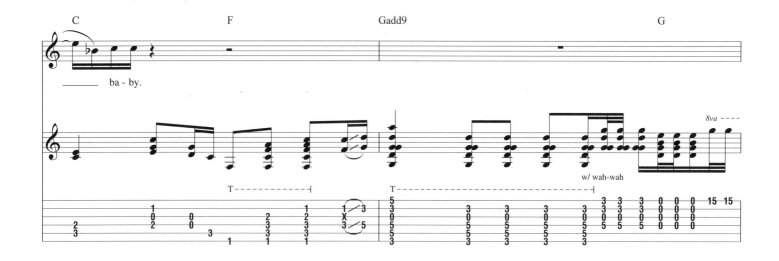

ba - by.

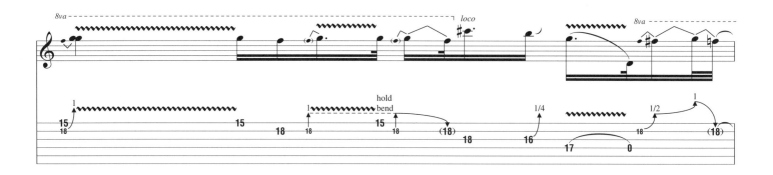

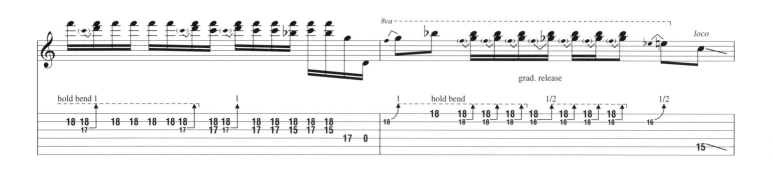

Free time

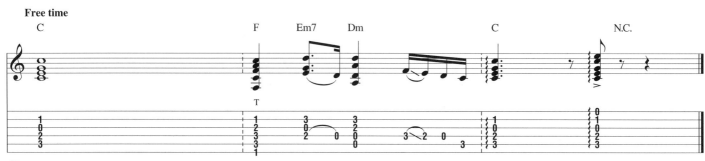

Hey Joe

Words and Music by Billy Roberts

Tune down 1/2 step:
(low to high) E♭-A♭-D♭-G♭-B♭-E♭

10/11/68 - 2nd show

Intro
Moderately slow ♩ = 76

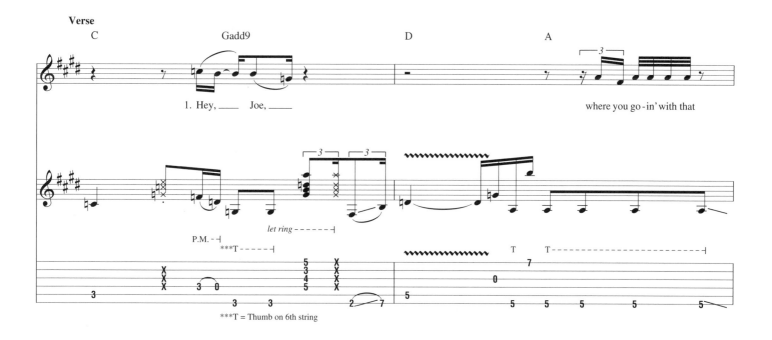

*Dist. generated solely by amp unless otherwise indicated.

**Chord symbols reflect basic harmony.

Verse

***T = Thumb on 6th string

gun in your hand?

*2nd string sounded by pull-off; don't pick.

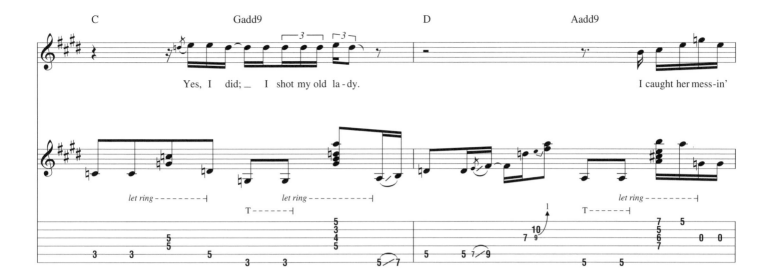

Yes, I did; ___ I shot my old la-dy. I caught her mess-in'

'round town. And you know I'm no fool, so I put the gun to her head. I shot her.

Guitar Solo

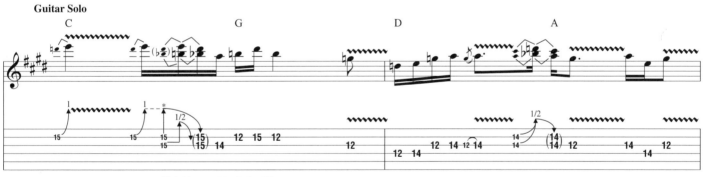

*3rd string caught under bend finger.

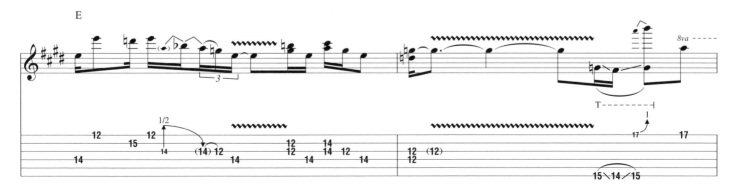

Interlude

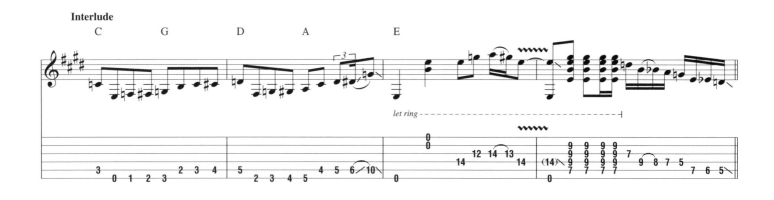

Verse

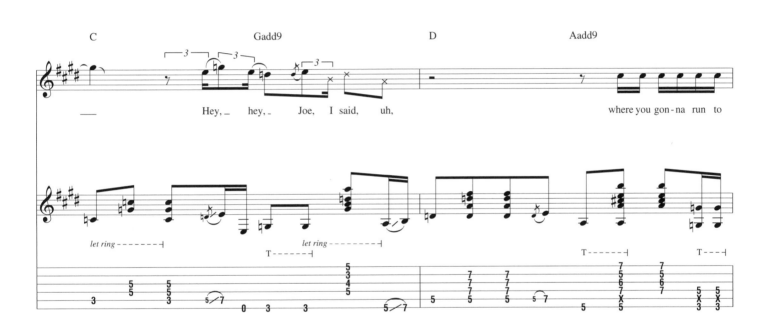

Hey, ___ hey, _ Joe, _ what you gon-na do?   Bet-ter make it on down real _

___quick, ba - by.   Yeah. _

Guitar Solo

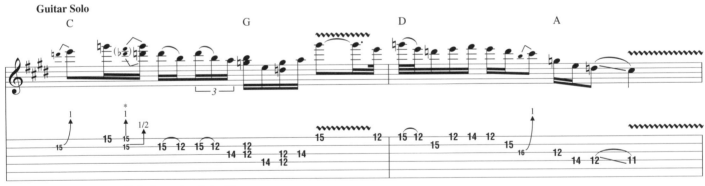

*2nd string caught under bend finger.

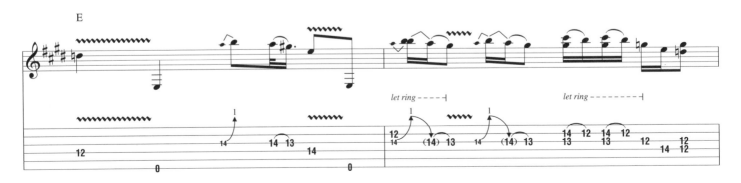

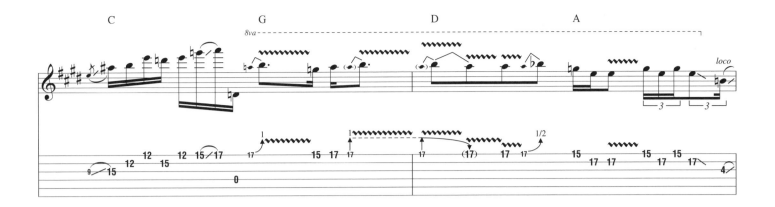

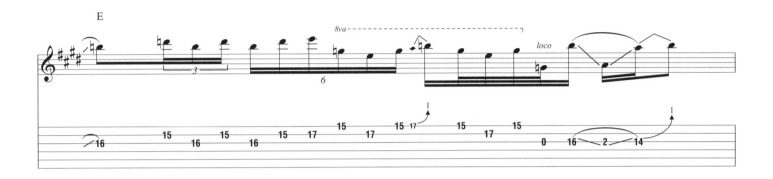

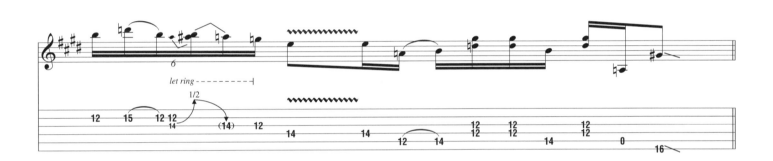

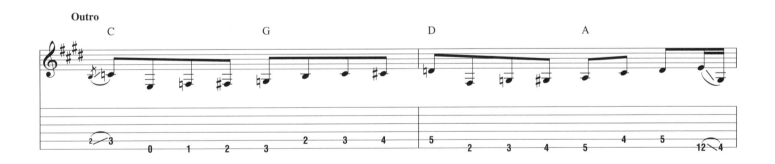

Outro

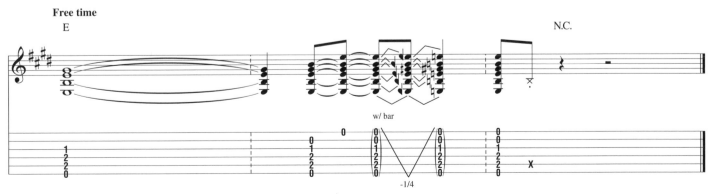

Hear My Train a Comin'

Words and Music by Jimi Hendrix

Tune down 1/2 step:
(low to high) E♭-A♭-D♭-G♭-B♭-E♭

10/10/68 - 2nd show

Intro
Moderately slow ♩ = 76

N.C.

*Gtr. 1 (dist.)

**mf

***w/ wah-wah

*Dist. generated solely by amp unless otherwise indicated.
**Roll back vol. knob halfway.
***Used as filter.

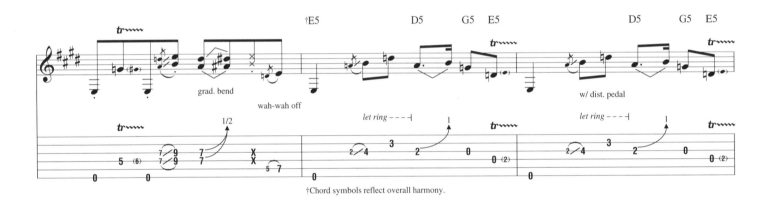

†Chord symbols reflect overall harmony.

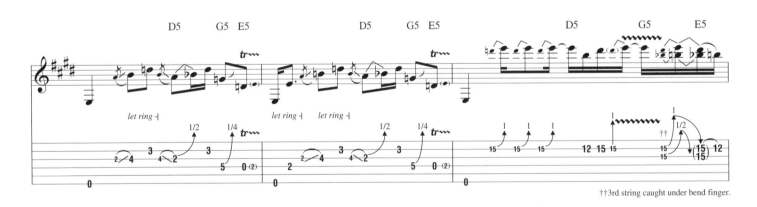

††3rd string caught under bend finger.

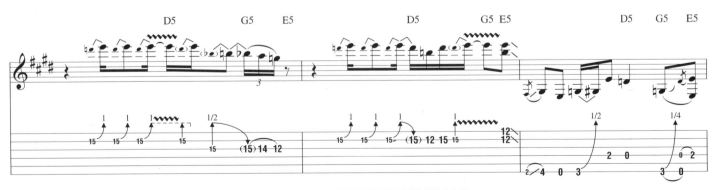

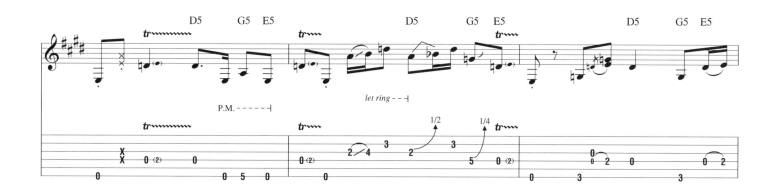

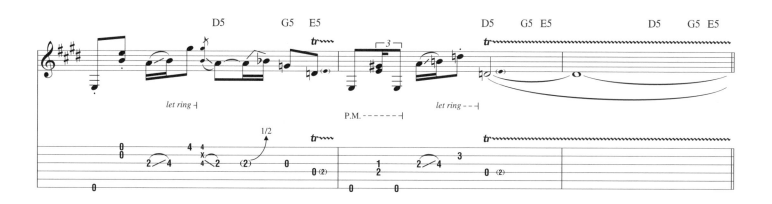

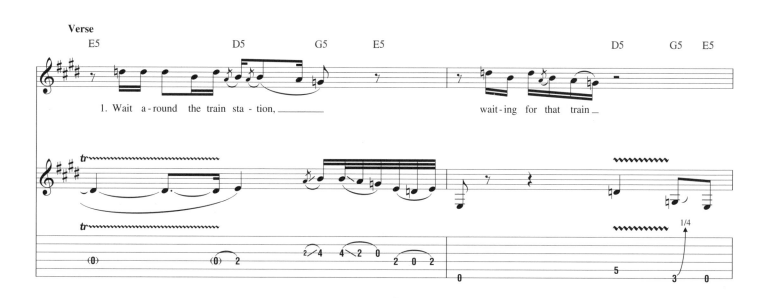

1. Wait a-round the train sta - tion, waiting for that train

to take me, take me a - way from this, uh, lone-some town.

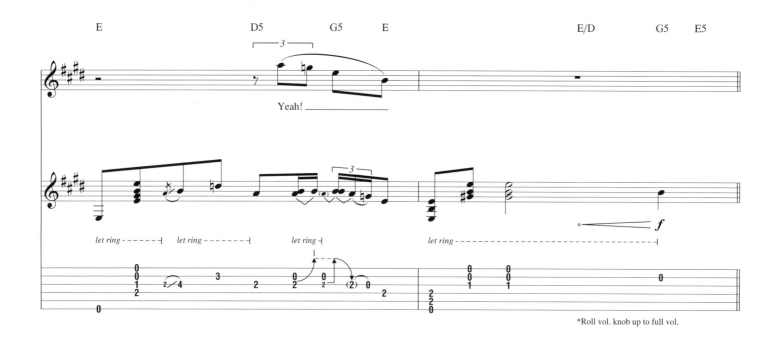

*Roll vol. knob up to full vol.

Chorus

Hear my train, _ a, com - in'. _

Hear my train, _ a, com - in'. _

Hear my train, _ a, com - in'. _

Hear my train, _ a, com - in'. _

Guitar Solo

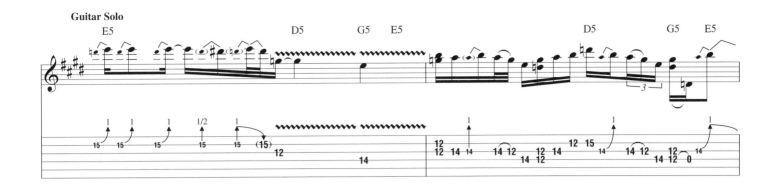

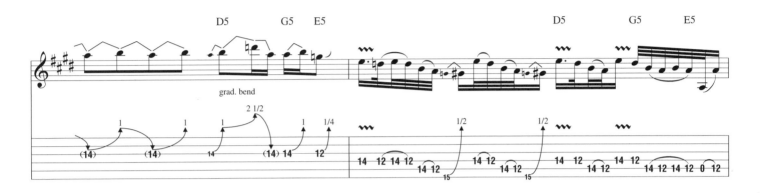

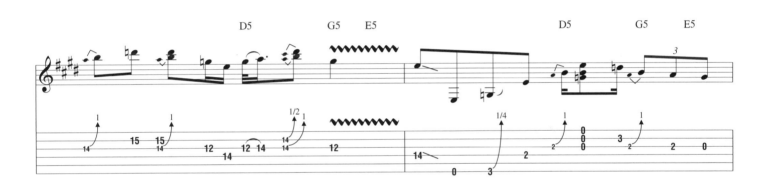

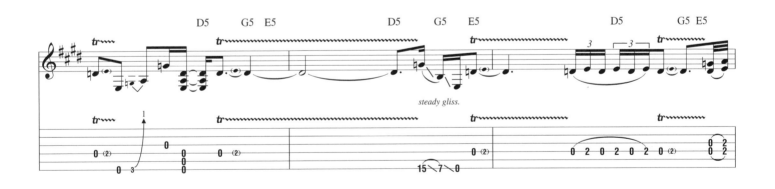

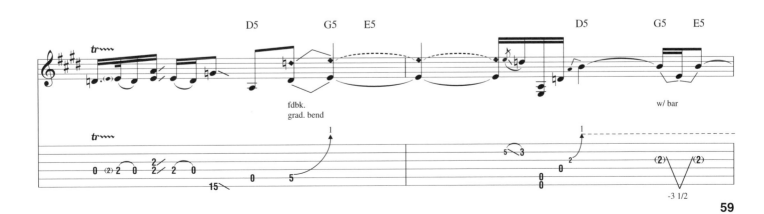

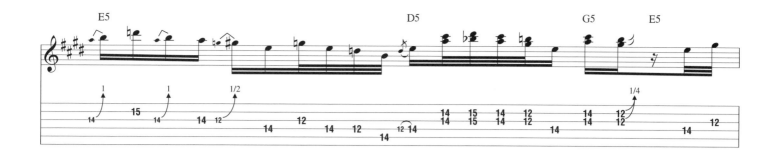

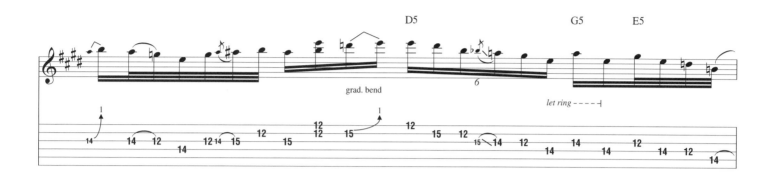

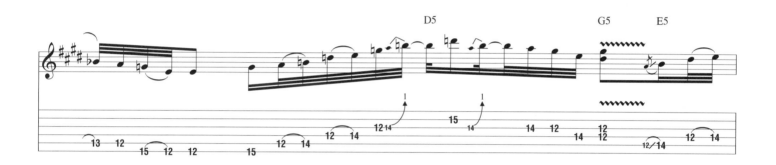

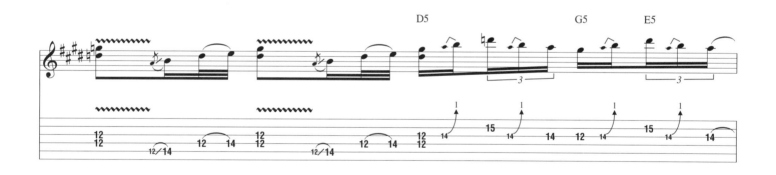

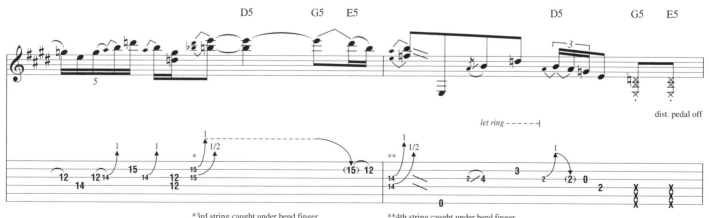

*3rd string caught under bend finger.   **4th string caught under bend finger.

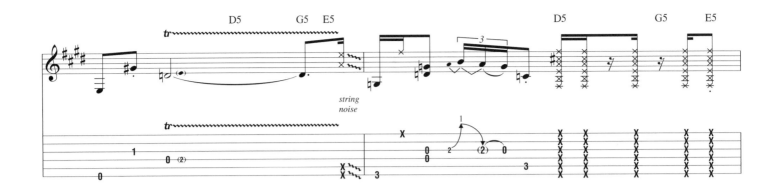

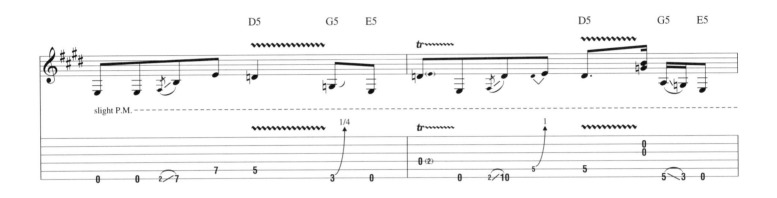

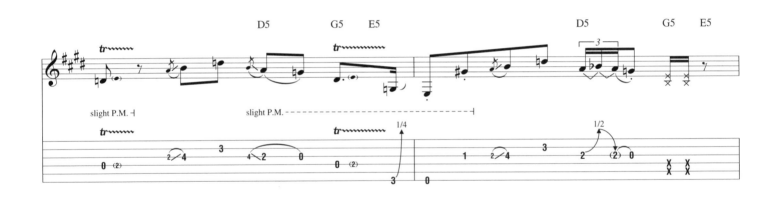

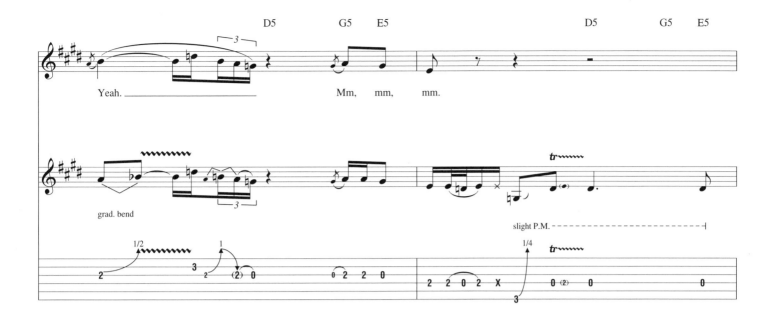

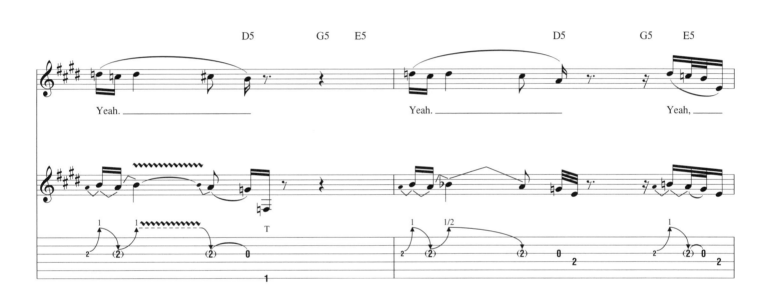

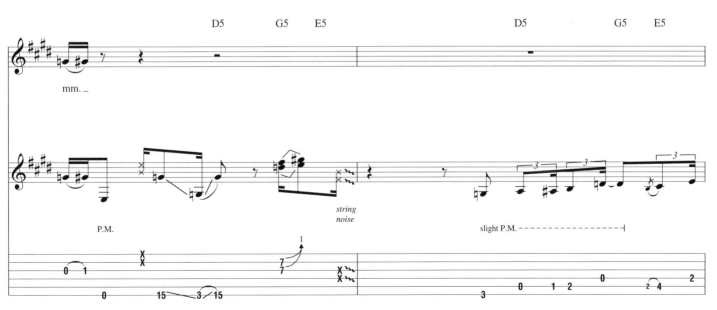

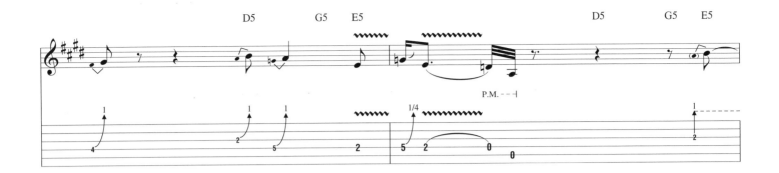

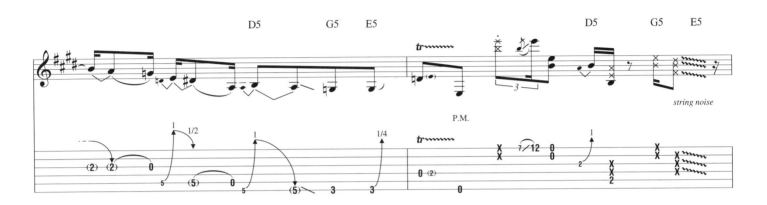

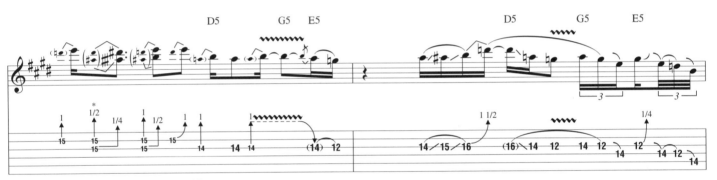

*3rd string caught under bend finger.

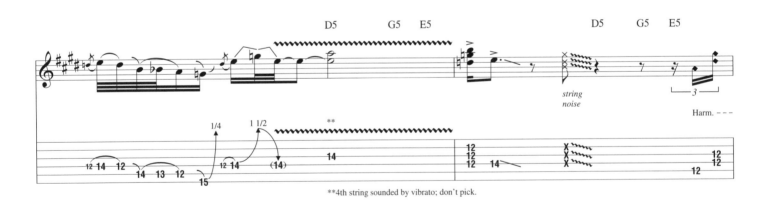

**4th string sounded by vibrato; don't pick.

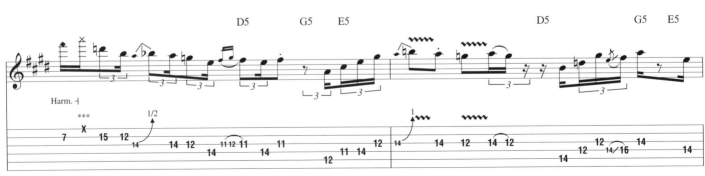

***Push string into pickup.

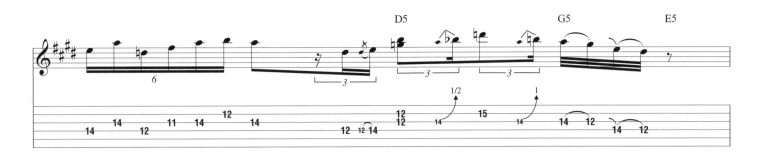

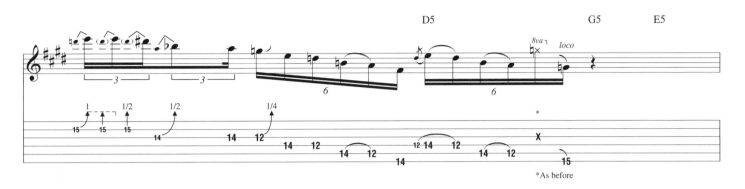

*As before

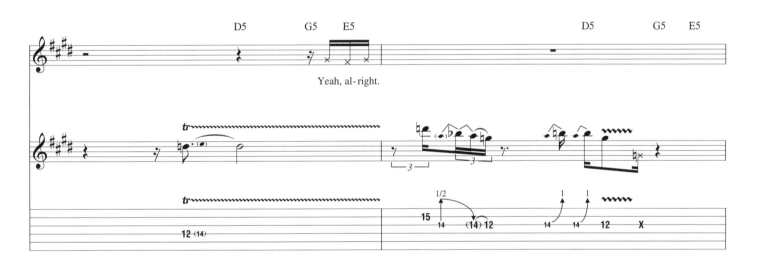

Yeah, al-right.

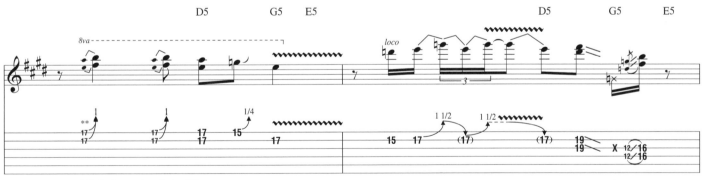

**2nd string caught under bend finger.

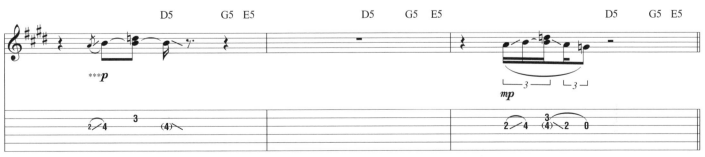

***Adjust vol. w/ knob (next 3 meas.).

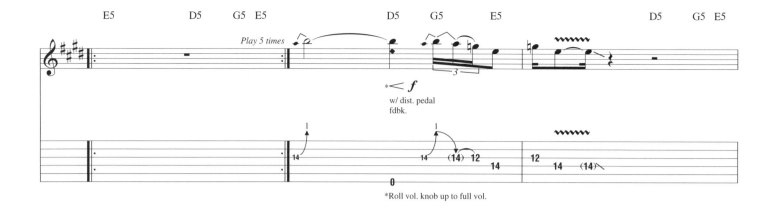

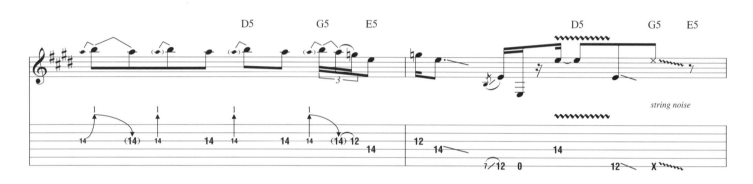

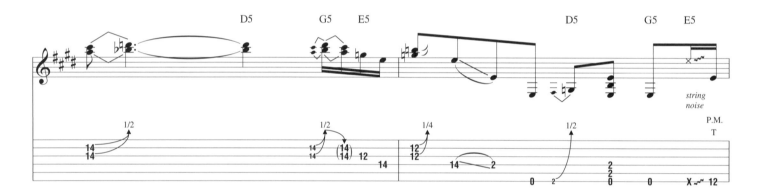

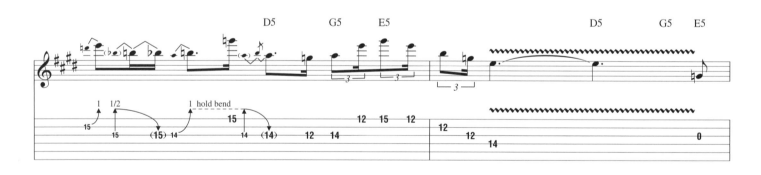

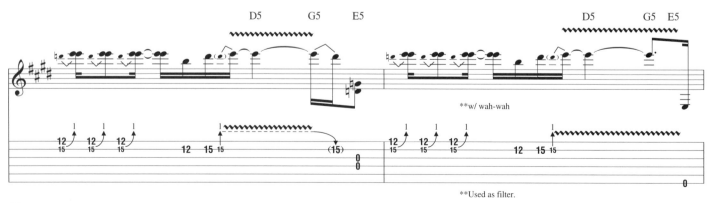

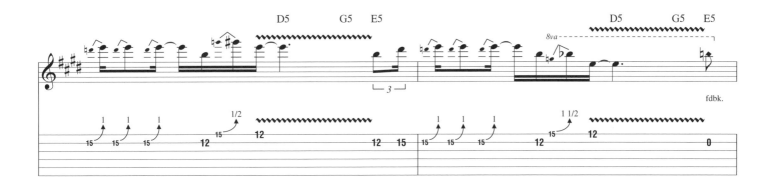

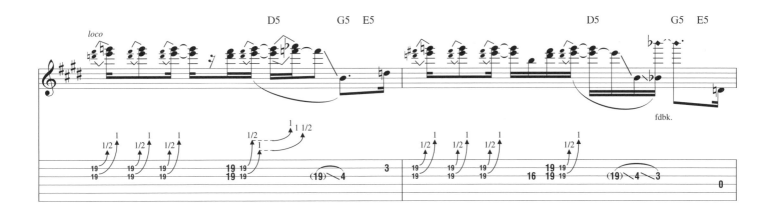

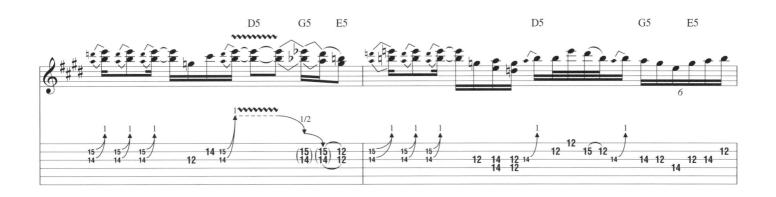

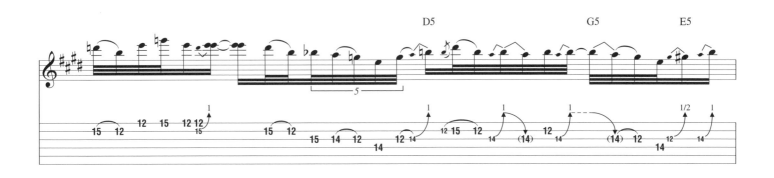

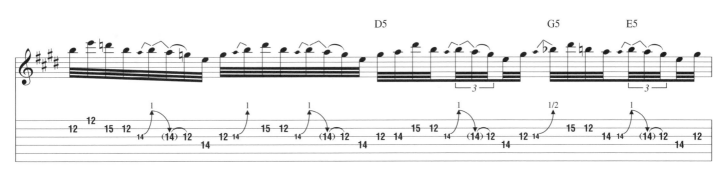

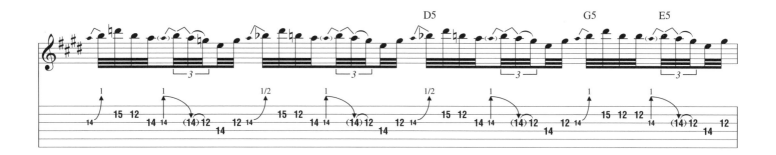

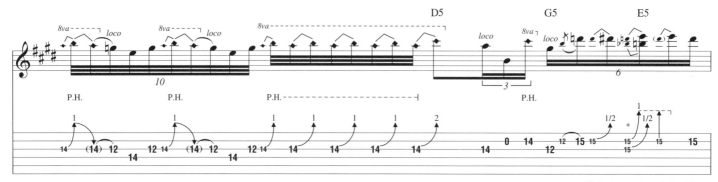

*3rd string caught under bend finger.

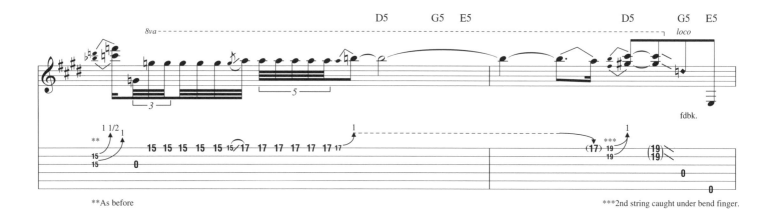

**As before

***2nd string caught under bend finger.

†Don't pick. Simulate re-attack by flipping toggle switch in rhythm indicated.

†††Set wah-wah pedal to open position (toe up).

††Roll back vol. knob halfway.

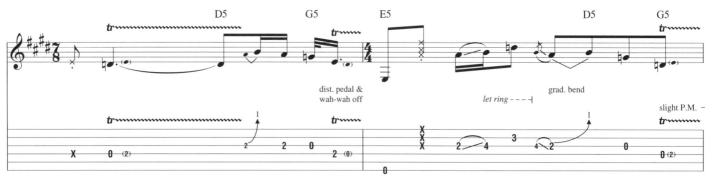

Guitar Solo

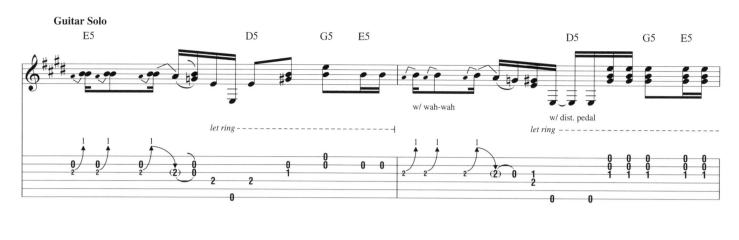

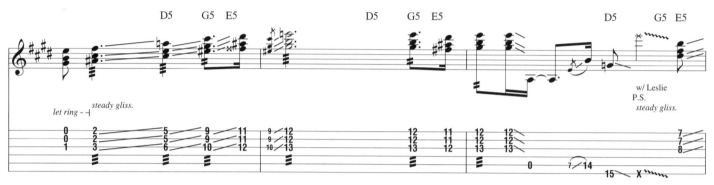

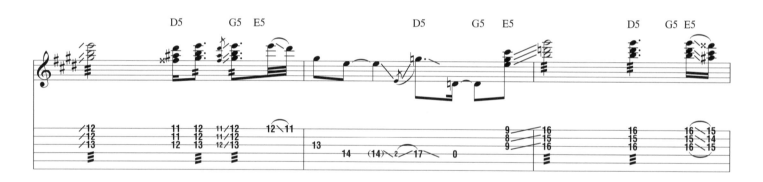

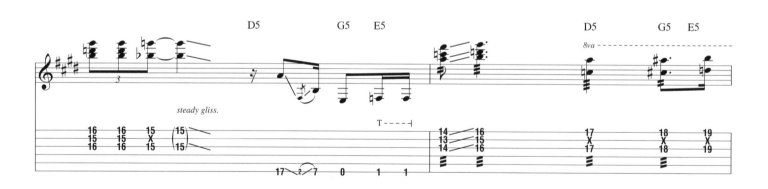

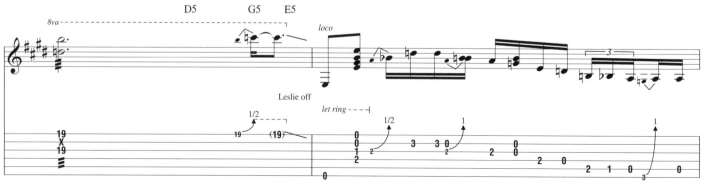

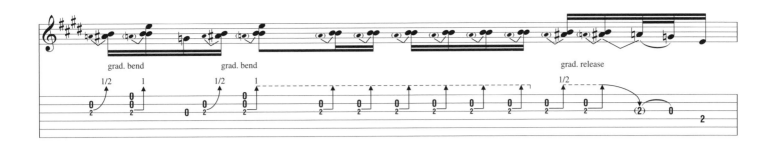

Outro
Free time

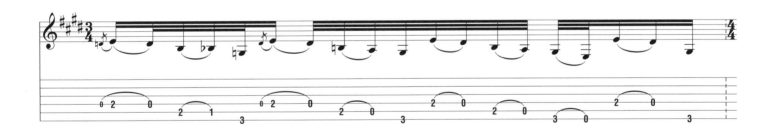

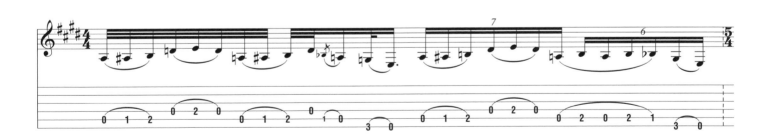

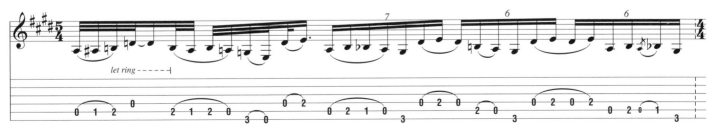

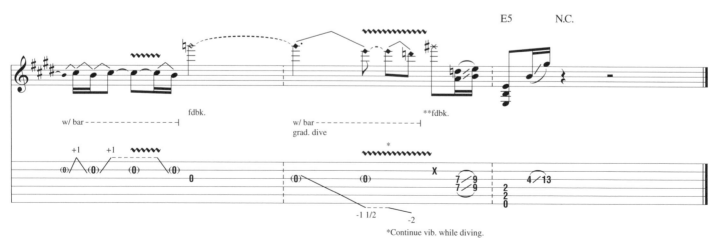

*Continue vib. while diving.

**Microphonic fdbk., not caused by string vibration.

Sunshine of Your Love

Words and Music by Jack Bruce, Pete Brown and Eric Clapton

Tune down 1/2 step:
(low to high) Eb-Ab-Db-Gb-Bb-Eb

10/10/68 - 2nd show

*T = Thumb on 6th string

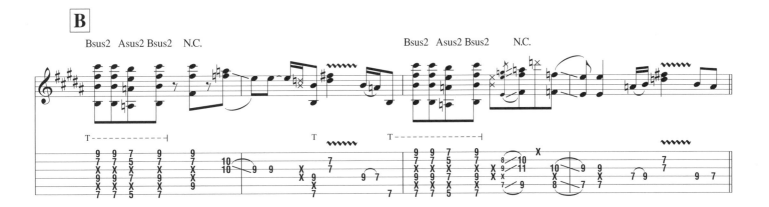

**Wah-wah indications: + = pedal closed (toe down); ○ = pedal open (toe up).

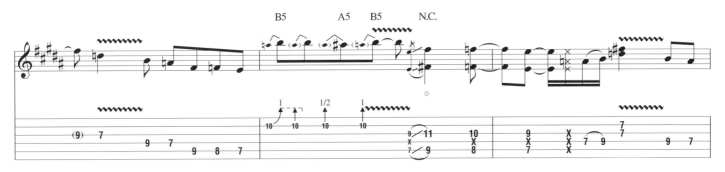

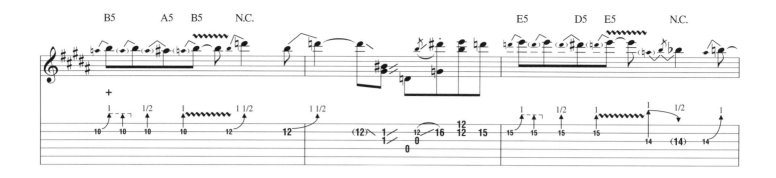

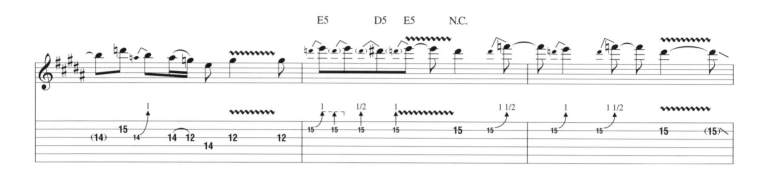

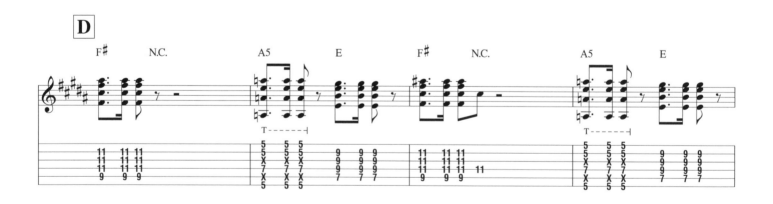

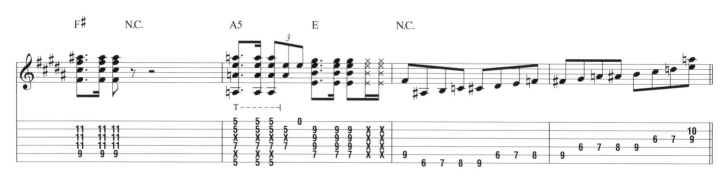

E

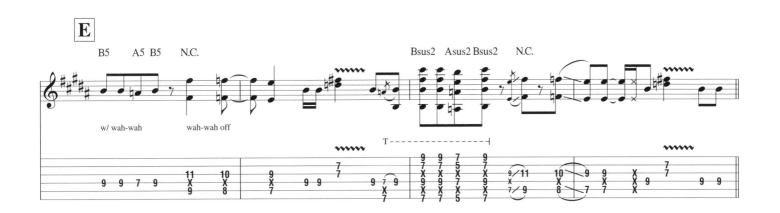

F

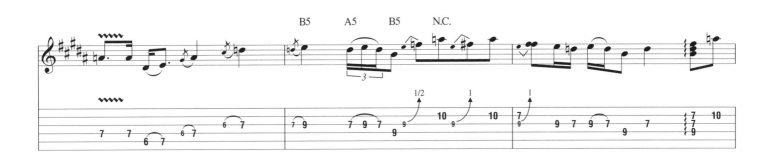

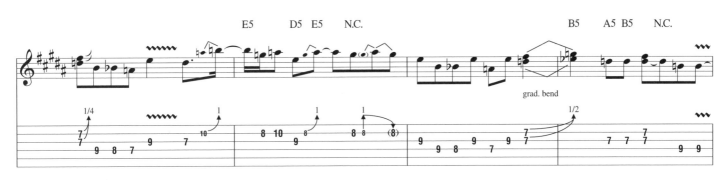

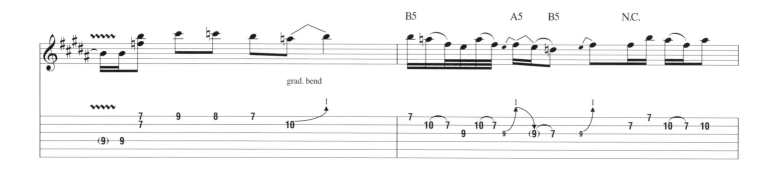

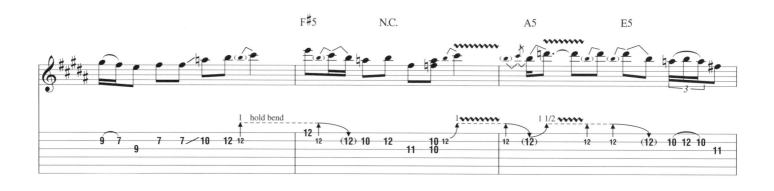

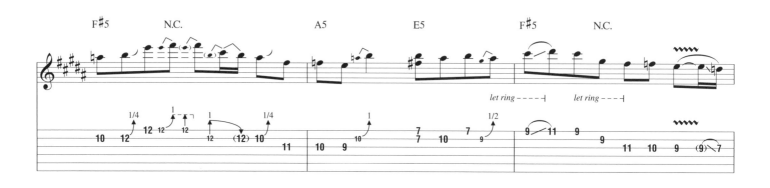

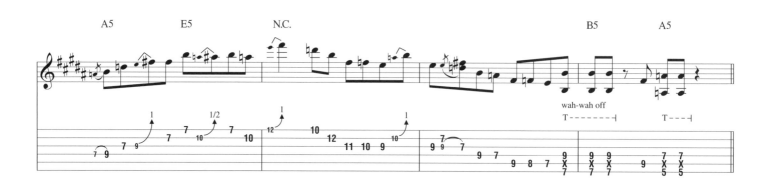

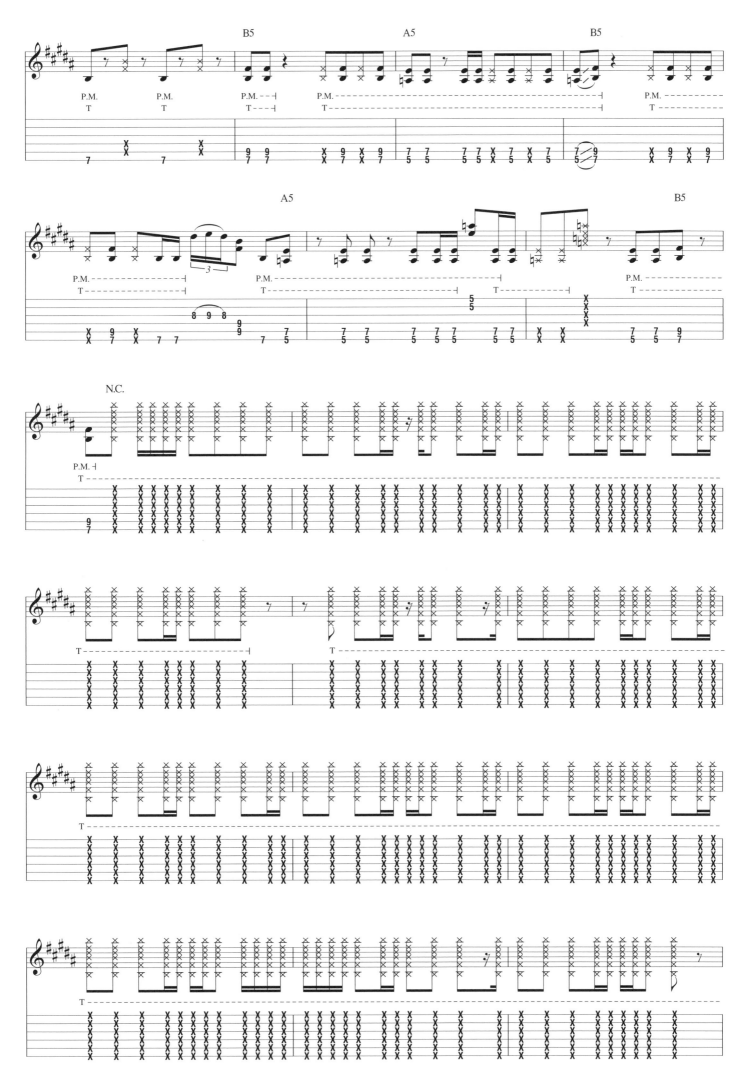

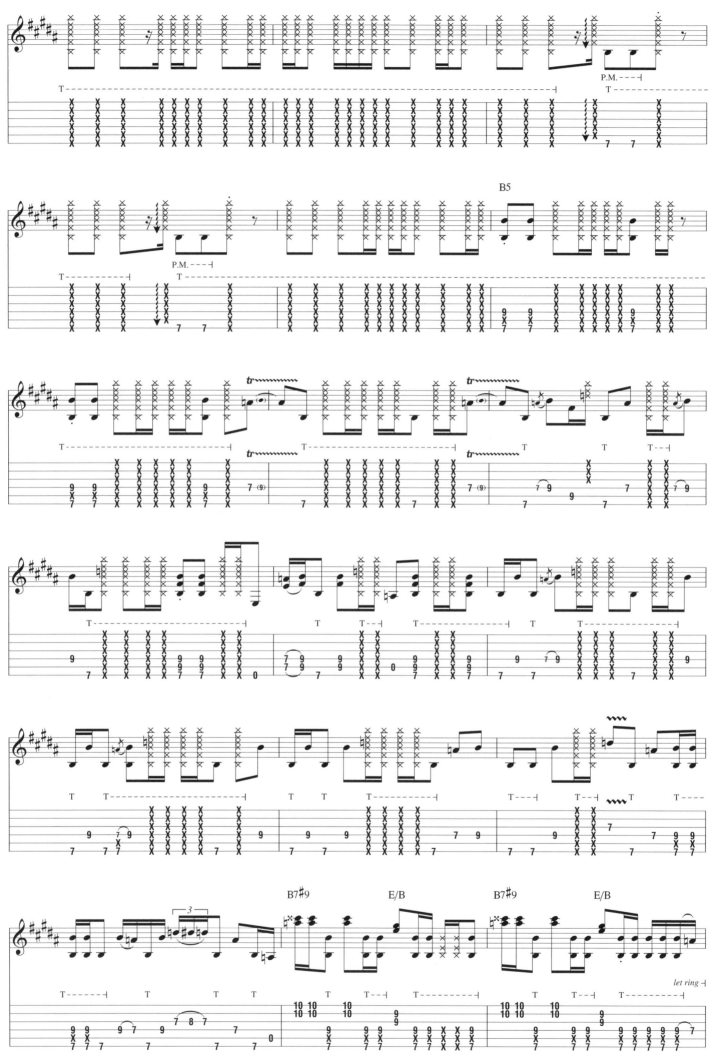

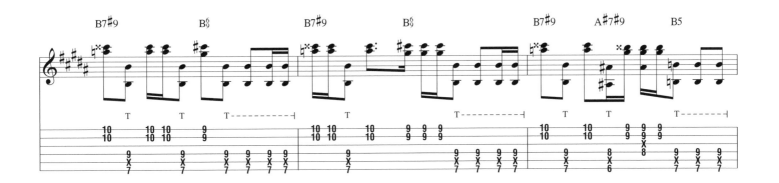

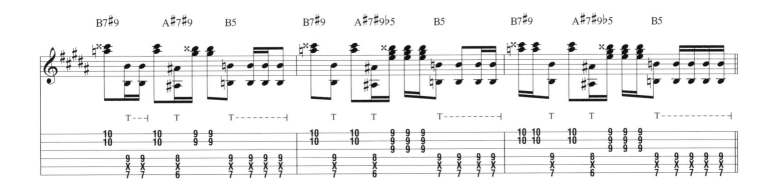

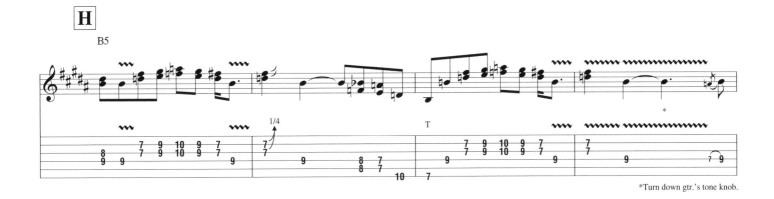

*Turn down gtr.'s tone knob.

**Turn gtr.'s tone knob back up.

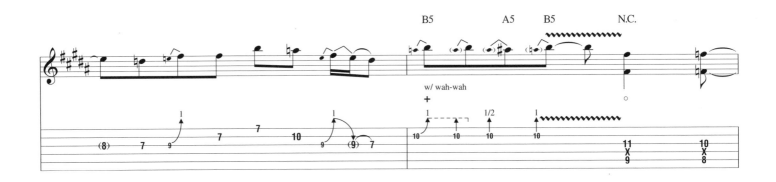

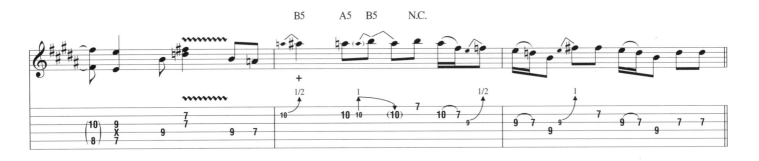

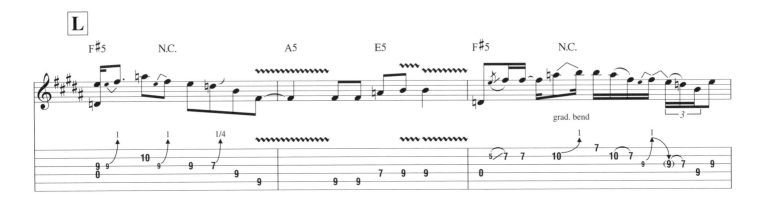

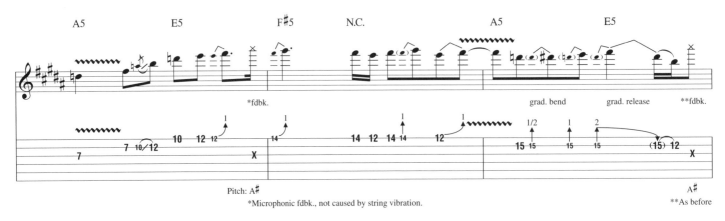

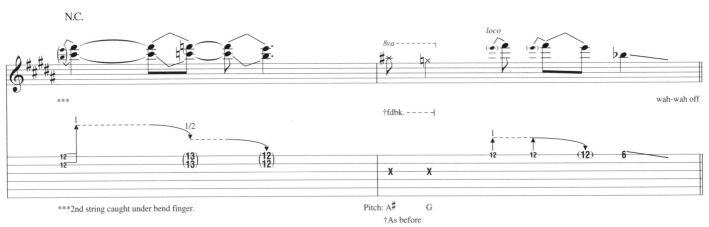

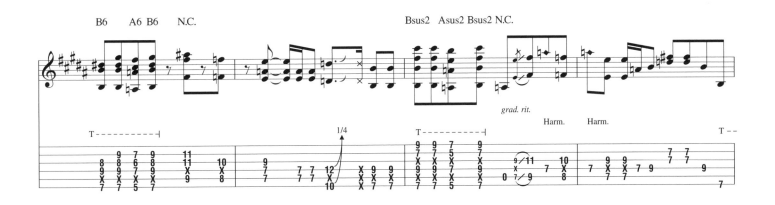

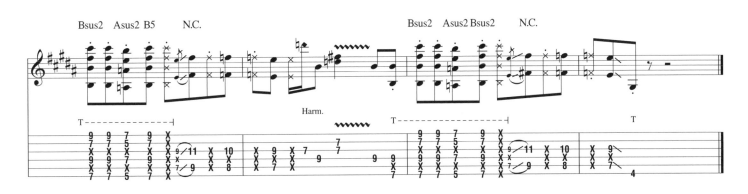

Little Wing

Words and Music by Jimi Hendrix

Tune down 1/2 step:
(low to high) E♭-A♭-D♭-G♭-B♭-E♭

10/12/68 - 2nd show

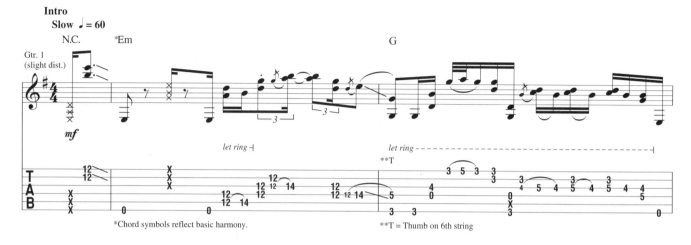

*Chord symbols reflect basic harmony.

**T = Thumb on 6th string

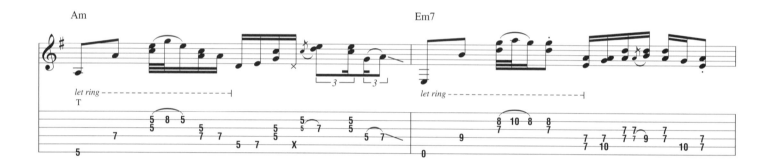

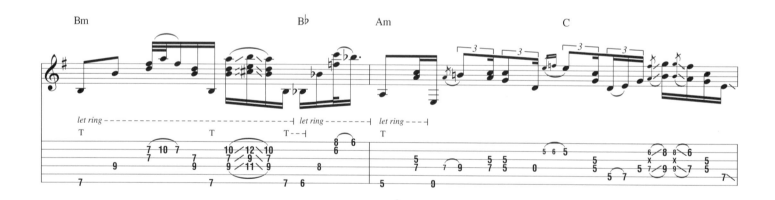

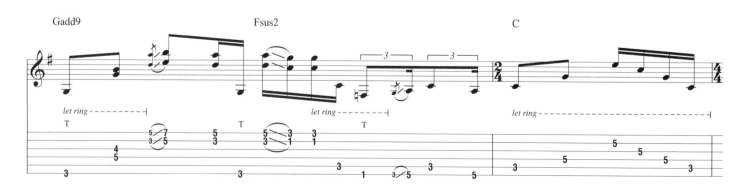

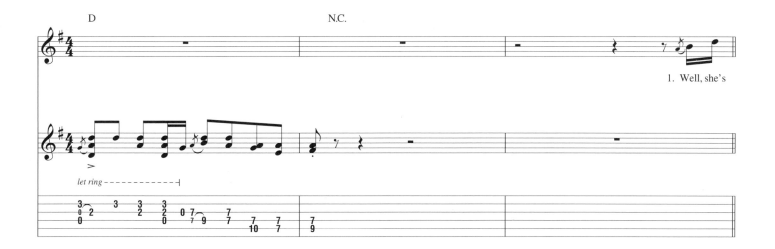

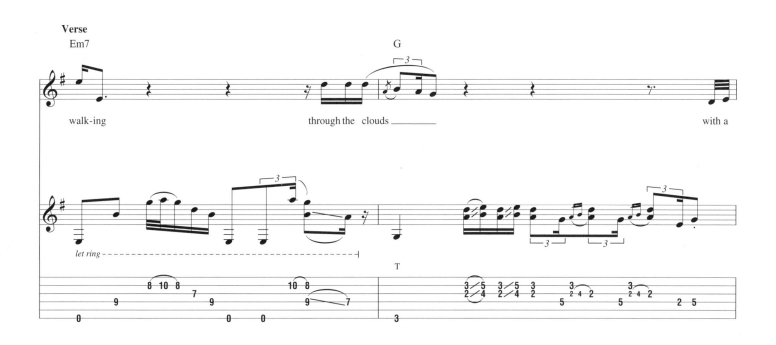

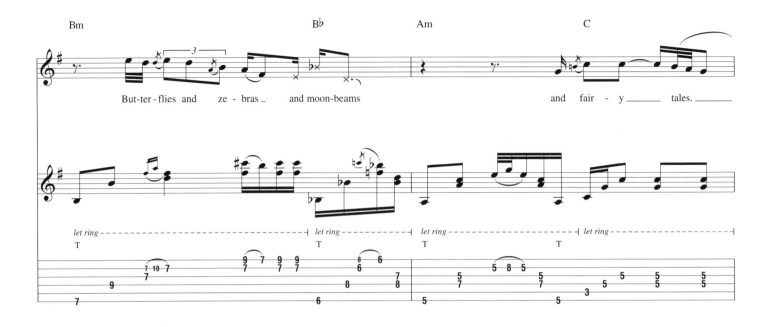

But-ter-flies and ze-bras and moon-beams and fair-y tales.

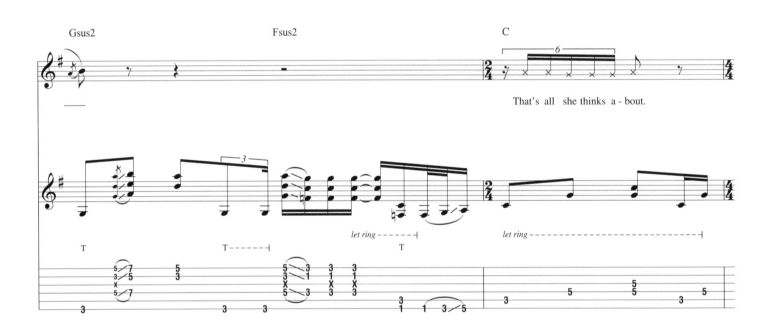

That's all she thinks a-bout.

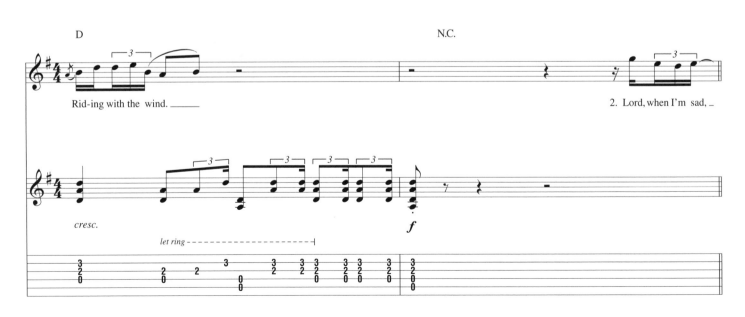

Rid-ing with the wind. 2. Lord, when I'm sad,

Verse

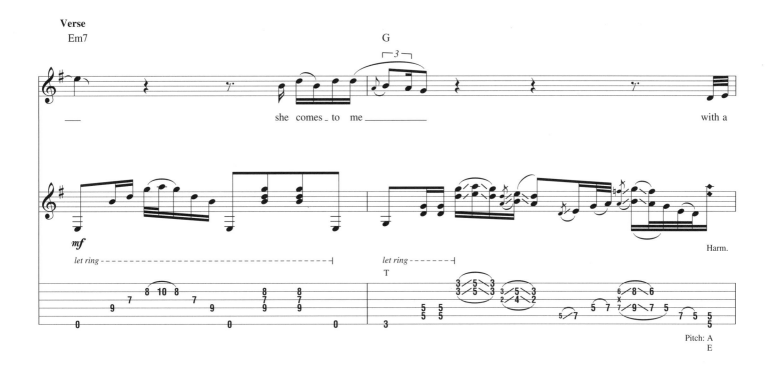

she comes to me _____ with a

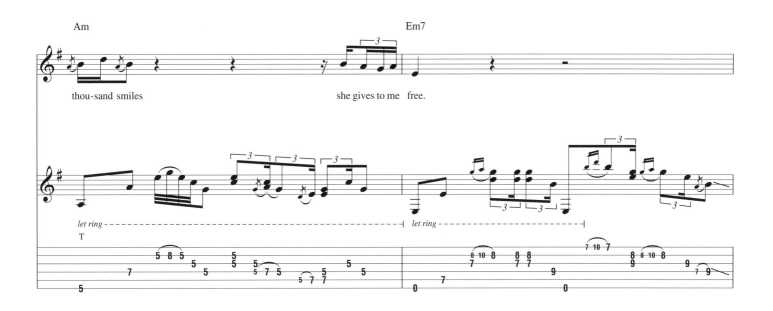

thou-sand smiles   she gives to me free.

"It's al - right, __ it's al - right," she says, _____   "It's al - right,   take an - y - thing __ you   want __

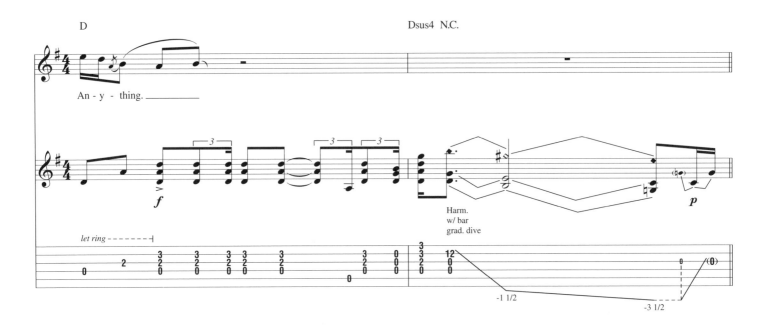

Guitar Solo

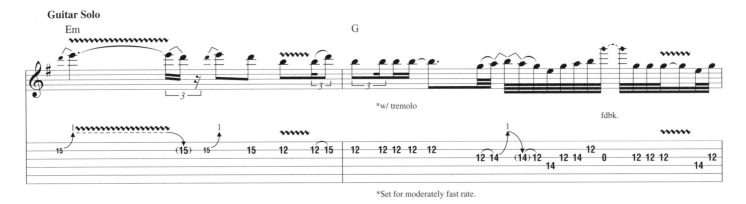

*Set for moderately fast rate.

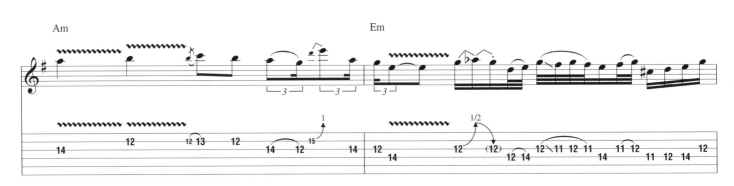

Bm   Am   C

tremolo off

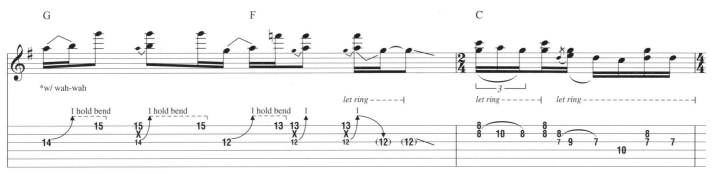

G   F   C

*w/ wah-wah

let ring

*Set pedal to midpoint till indicated.

D   N.C.

let ring

fdbk.
w/ bar
grad. dive   grad. ascent

Pitch: D

**Rock wah-wah pedal back and forth.

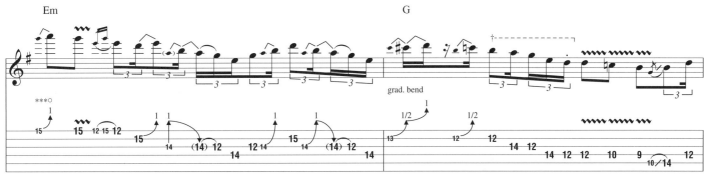

Em   G

grad. bend

***○

***Wah-wah indications:○ = pedal open (toe up); ✛ = pedal closed (toe down).   †Played behind the beat.

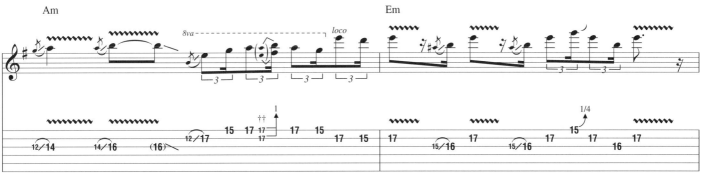

Am   Em

8va   loco

††Catch and bend both strings w/ ring finger.

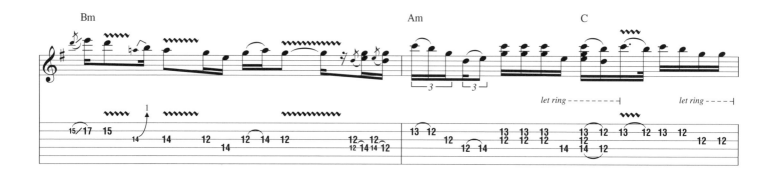

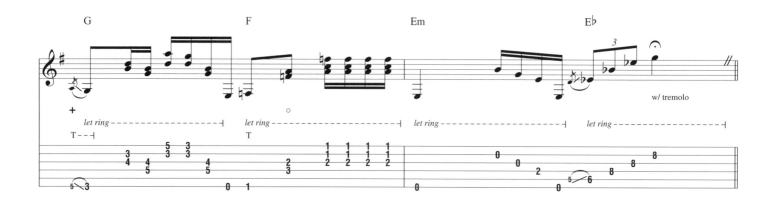

Outro
Free time

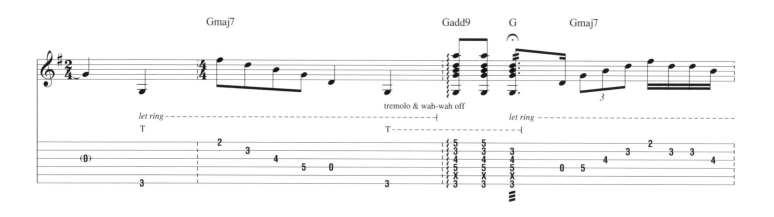

Are You Experienced?

Words and Music by Jimi Hendrix

Tune down 1/2 step:
(low to high) Eb-Ab-Db-Gb-Bb-Eb

10/10/68 - 1st show

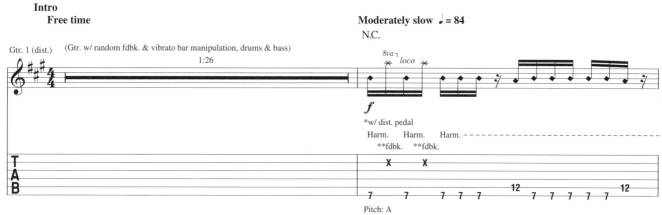

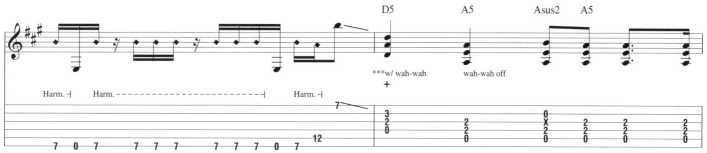

†Chord symbols reflect implied harmony.
Bass plays A pedal throughout all verses.

††T = Thumb on 6th string

Verse

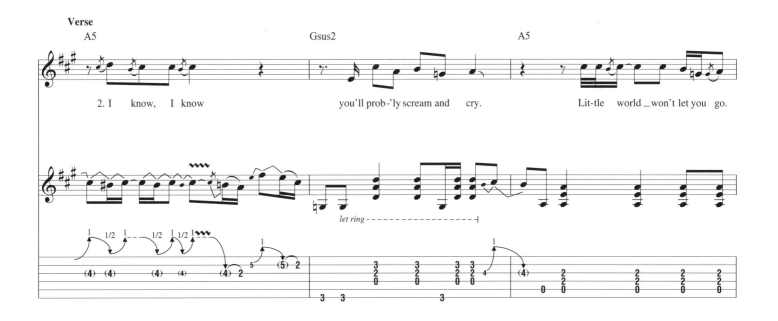

2. I know, I know you'll prob-'ly scream and cry. Lit-tle world _ won't let you go.

let ring

But who in your meas-ly lit-tle world

dist. pedal off

w/ bar

*Lift index finger slightly to stop 4th string from ringing, then re-fret on beat 4 without picking. Re-attack simulated by bar.

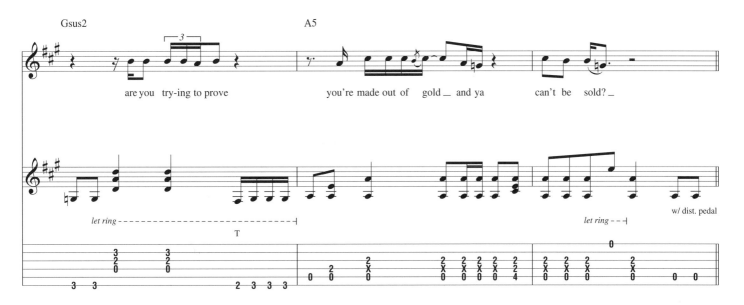

are you try-ing to prove you're made out of gold _ and ya can't be sold? _

let ring

w/ dist. pedal

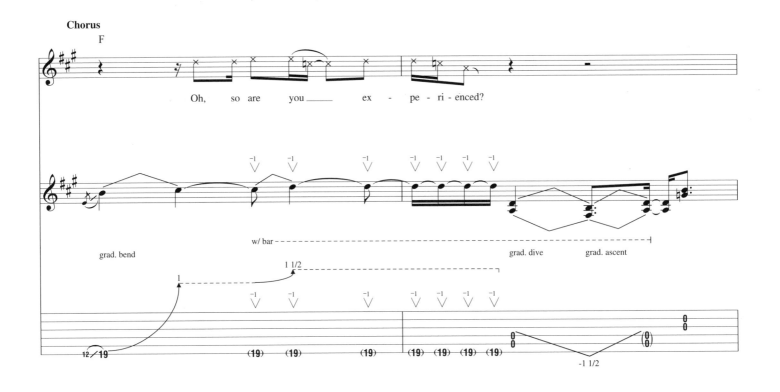

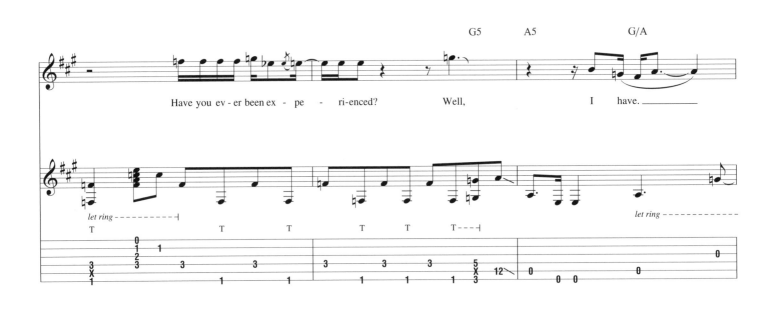

Guitar Solo

A5

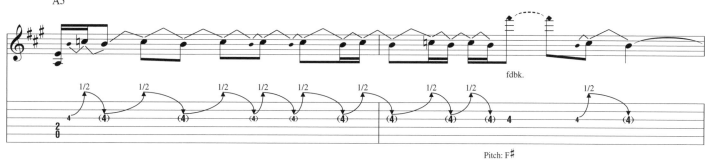

fdbk.

Pitch: F#

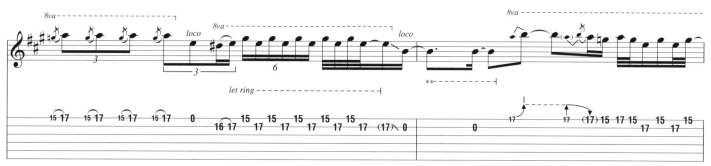

grad. release

w/ wah-wah

*Re-attack simulated by turning wah-wah pedal on; don't pick.

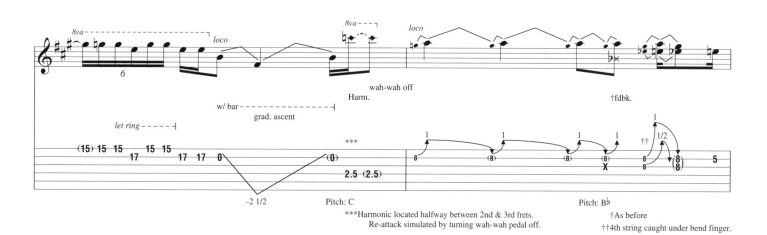

let ring

**Quickly rock wah-wah pedal back and forth, ending in closed position (toe down) as before.

wah-wah off
Harm.

†fdbk.

w/ bar
grad. ascent

let ring

Pitch: C

Pitch: B♭

***Harmonic located halfway between 2nd & 3rd frets. Re-attack simulated by turning wah-wah pedal off.

†As before
††4th string caught under bend finger.

†††5th string caught under bend finger.

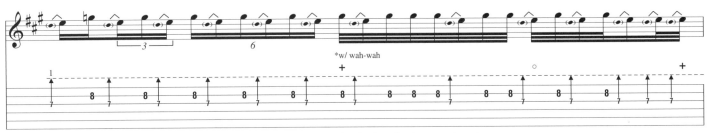

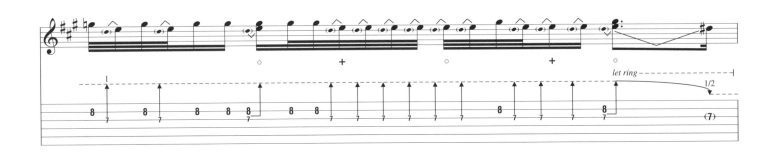

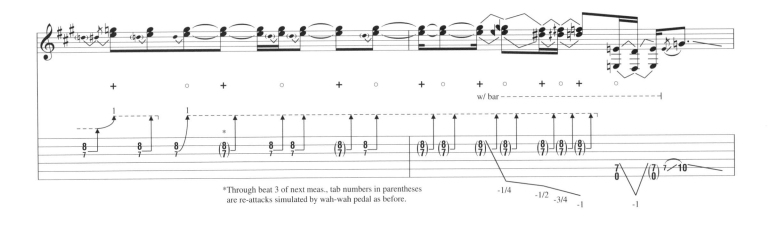

*Through beat 3 of next meas., tab numbers in parentheses
are re-attacks simulated by wah-wah pedal as before.

**Open string sounded by pull-off; don't pick.

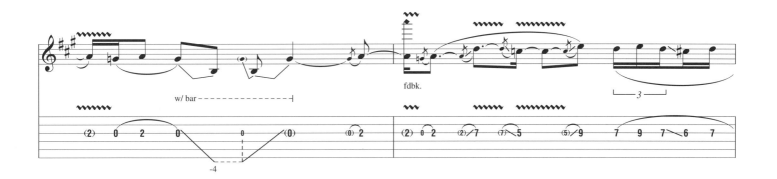

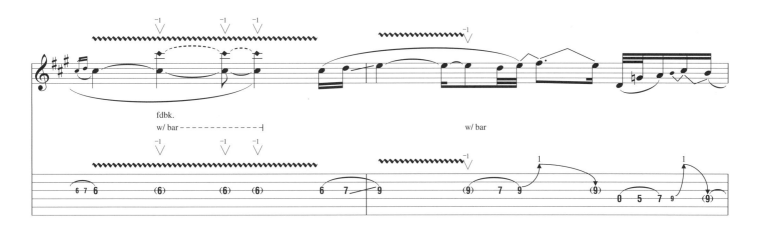

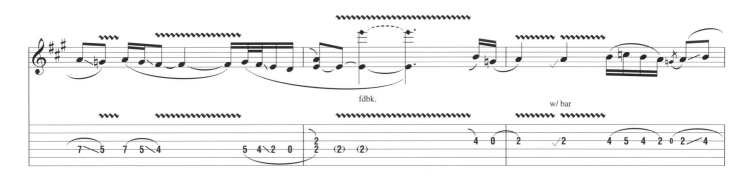

*2nd string sounded by pull-off; don't pick.

**Continue vib. w/ bar while releasing bend.

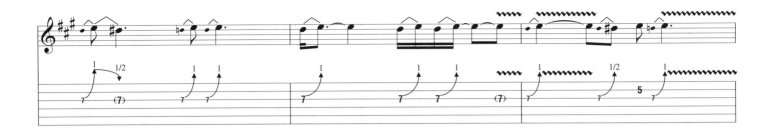

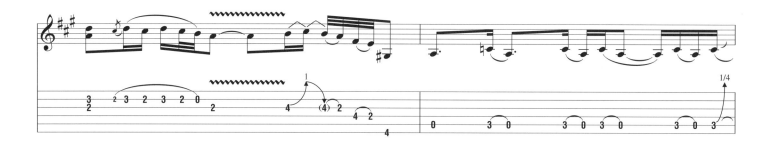

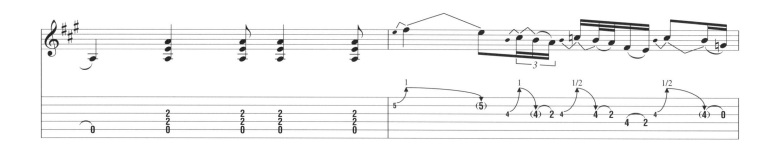

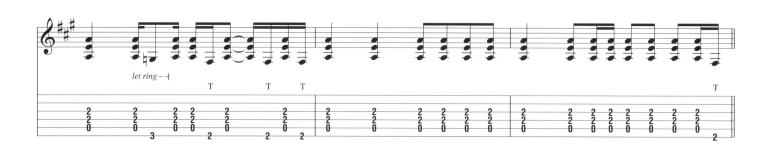

Outro

Free time

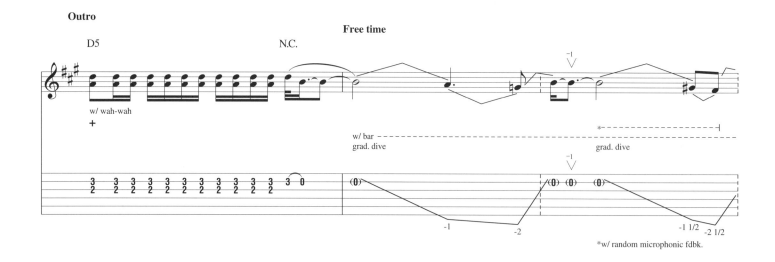

*w/ random microphonic fdbk.

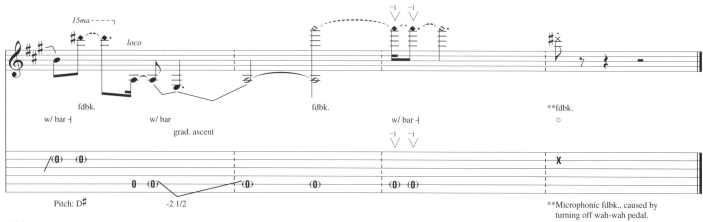

**Microphonic fdbk., caused by
turning off wah-wah pedal.

Manic Depression

Words and Music by Jimi Hendrix

Tune down 1/2 step:
(low to high) Eb-Ab-Db-Gb-Bb-Eb

10/12/68 - 2nd show

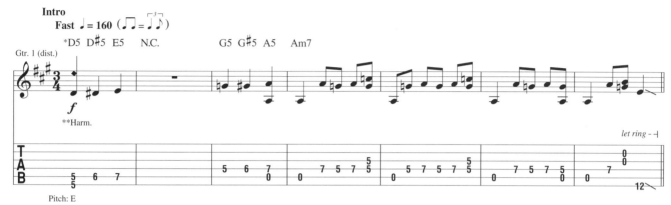

Pitch: E

*Chord symbols reflect implied harmony.

**Refers to 6th string only; which is lightly touched by thumb.

Verse

1. Man - ic de - pres - sion's touch - ing my soul. ___

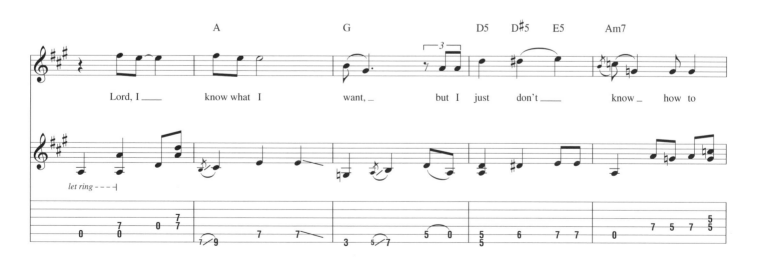

Lord, I ___ know what I want, ___ but I just don't ___ know ___ how to

Pitch: F#

*Microphonic fdbk., not caused by string vibration.

Interlude

A7(no3rd)

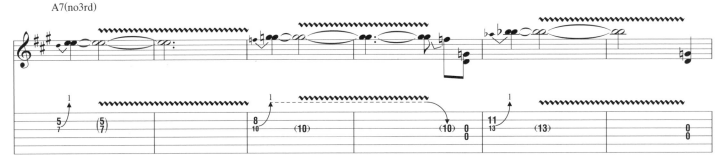

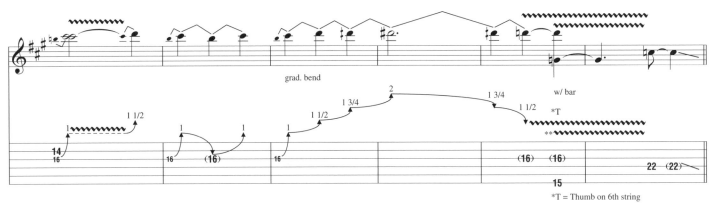

grad. bend

w/ bar

*T

**add vib. w/ bar while continuing hand vib.

*T = Thumb on 6th string
**Add vib. w/ bar while continuing hand vib.

Guitar Solo

A7(no3rd)

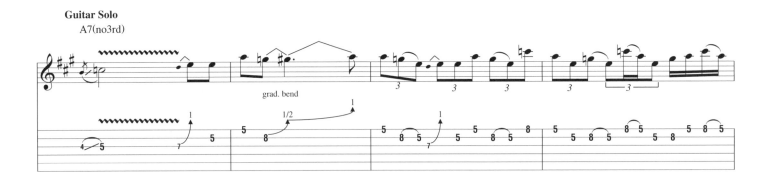

grad. bend

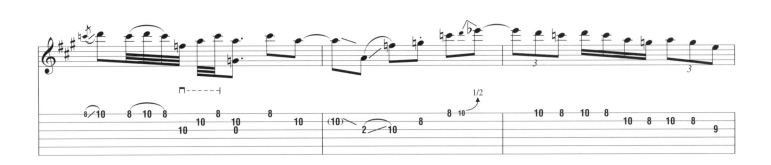

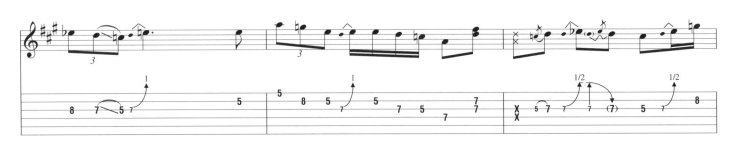

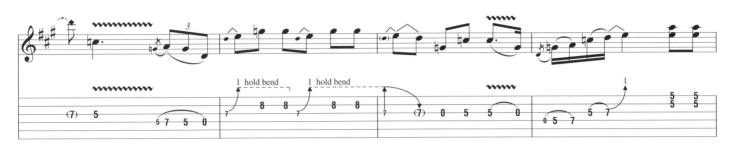

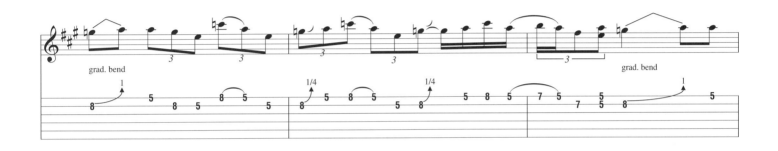

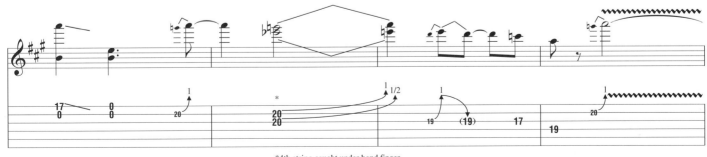

*4th string caught under bend finger.

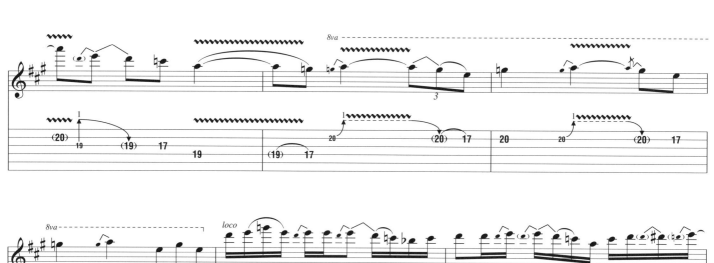

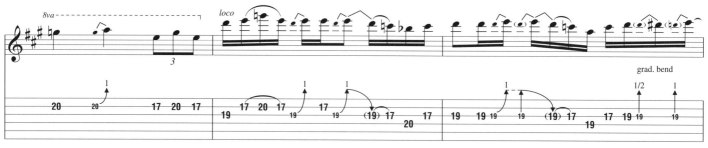

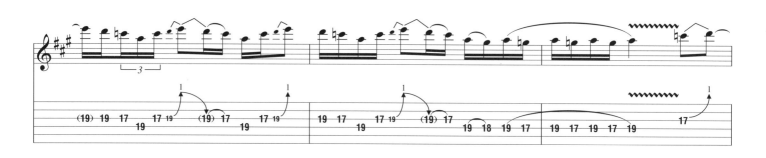

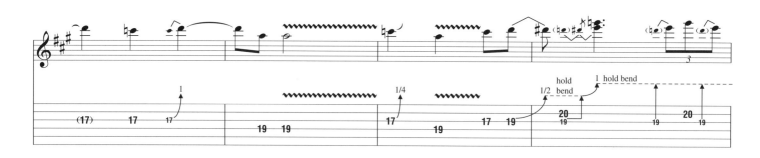

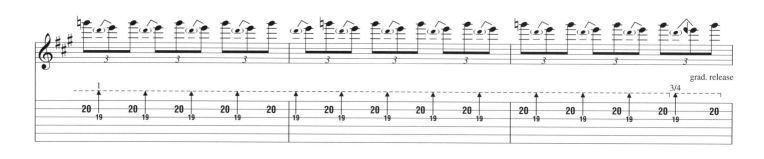

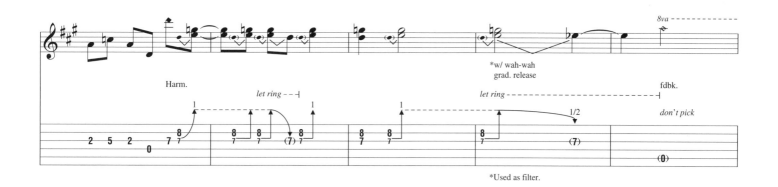

*w/ wah-wah
grad. release

*Used as filter.

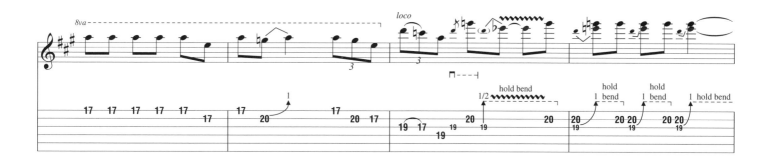

grad. bend

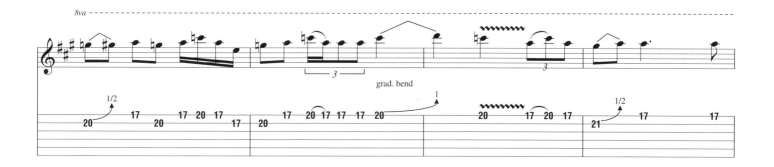

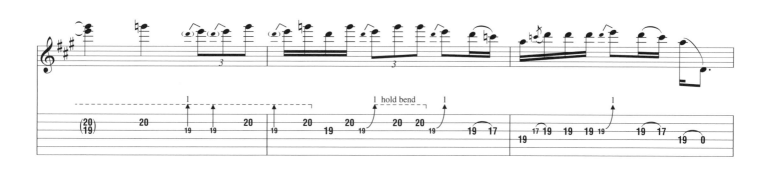

**Played as even eighth-notes.

***Played behind the beat.

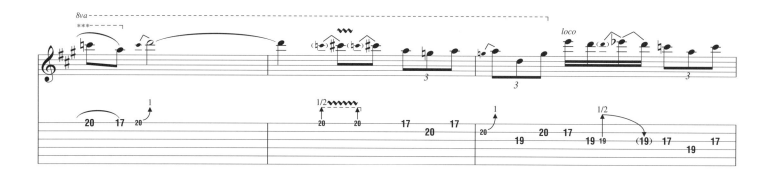

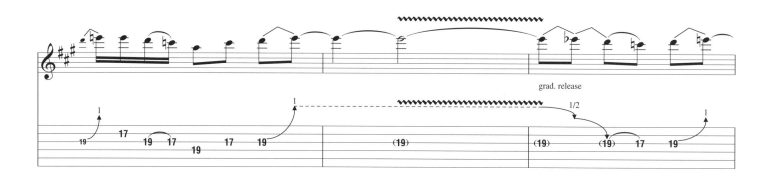

Cry on, gui - tar.

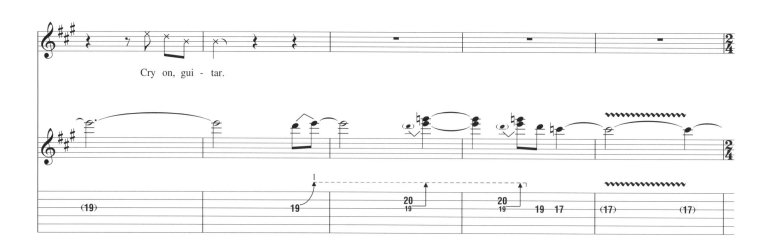

Verse

A   G   D5 D#5 E5   A7(no3rd)

3. Well, I ___ think I'll go turn my - self off ___ and go right on down.

wah-wah off

let ring - - - - - - -

Interlude

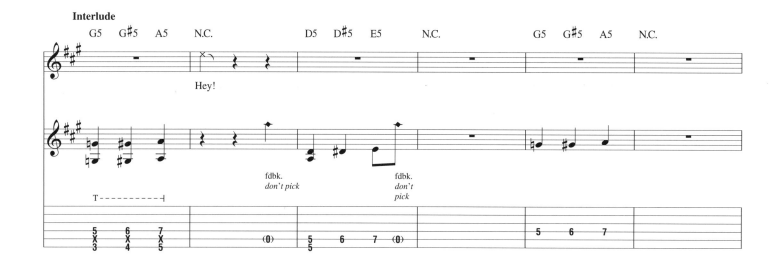

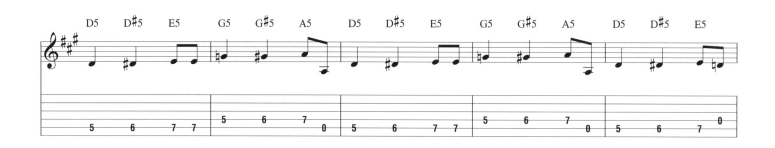

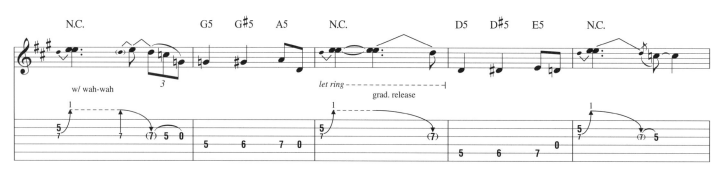

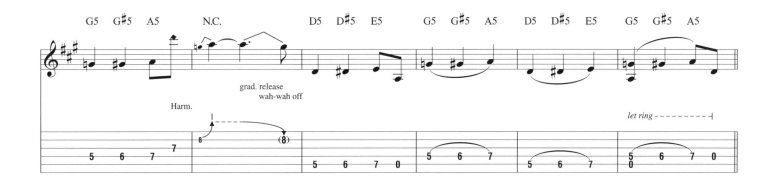

Outro

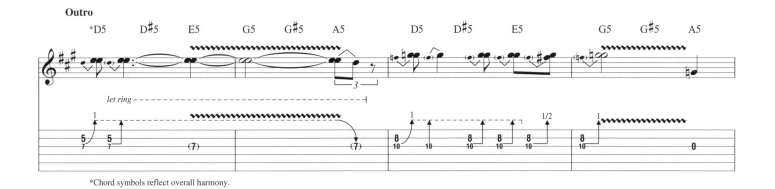

*Chord symbols reflect overall harmony.

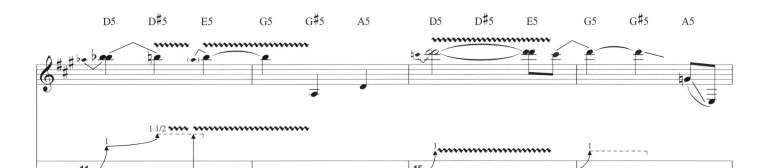

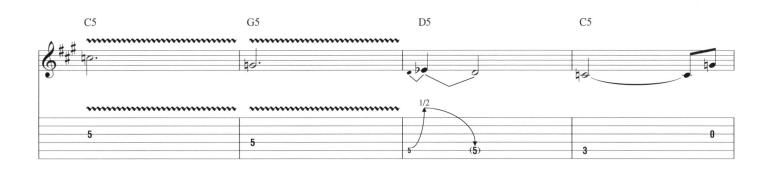

Free time

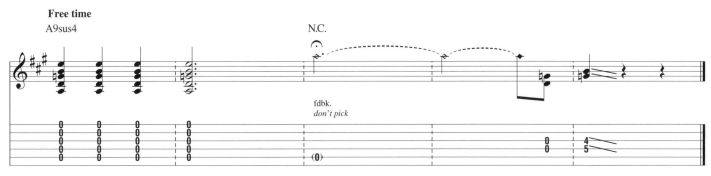

Voodoo Child (Slight Return)

Words and Music by Jimi Hendrix

Tune down 1/2 step:
(low to high) E♭-A♭-D♭-G♭-B♭-E♭

10/12/68 - 1st show

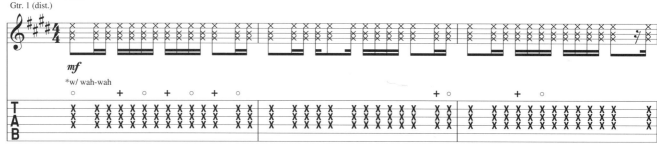

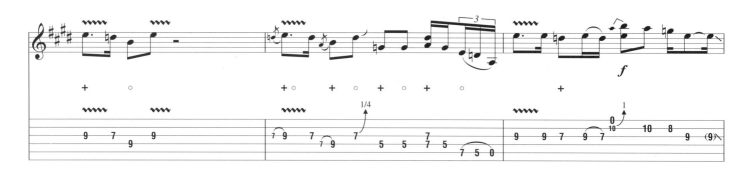

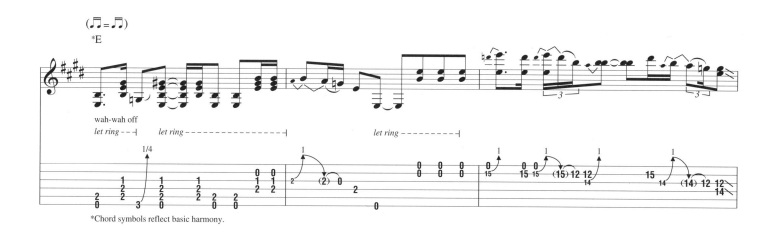

*E

wah-wah off

*Chord symbols reflect basic harmony.

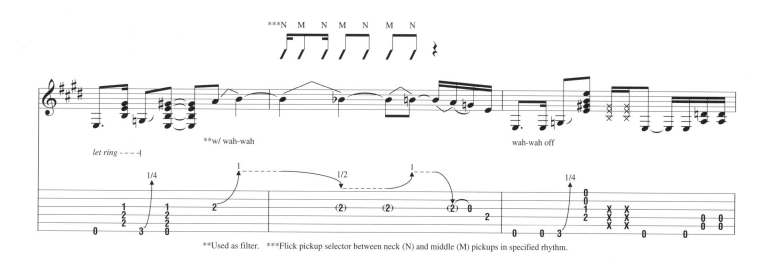

**w/ wah-wah

wah-wah off

**Used as filter.   ***Flick pickup selector between neck (N) and middle (M) pickups in specified rhythm.

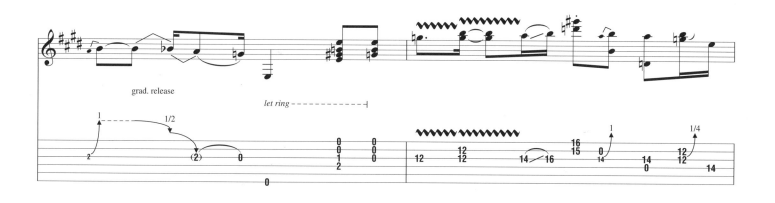

grad. release

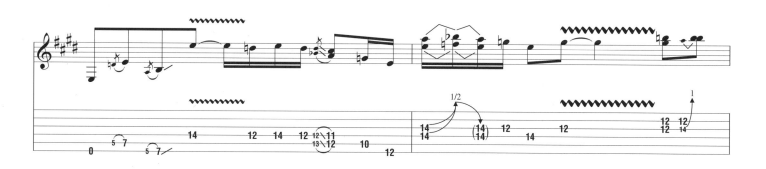

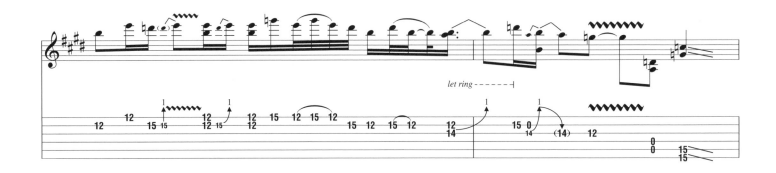

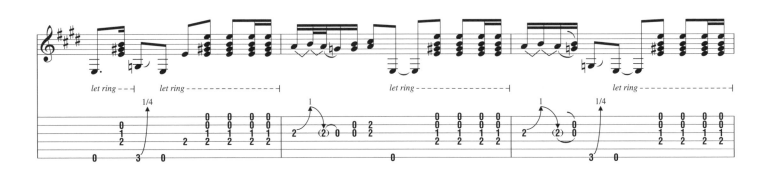

Verse

E

1. Well, I stand up next to a moun-tain, I chop it down with the edge of my

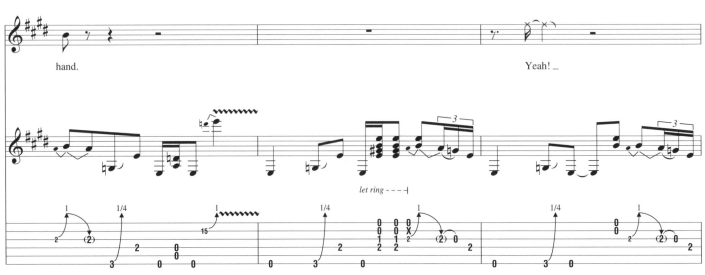

hand. Yeah! _

Well, I stand up next to a moun-tain, I chop it down ___ with the edge of my hand.

Well, I pick up all the piec-es and make an is - land,

might e - ven raise a lit - tle sand.

'Cause I'm a voo-doo child, ___ voo-doo child. ___

Lord   knows _ I'm a   voo-doo child, _   hey. ___

Guitar Solo

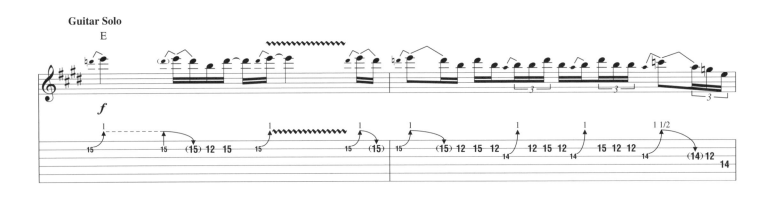

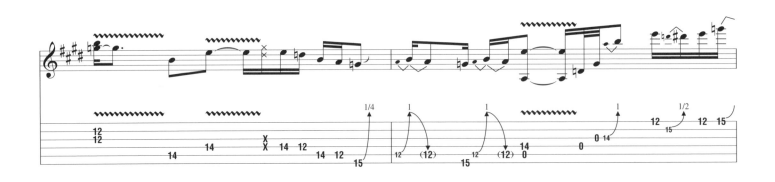

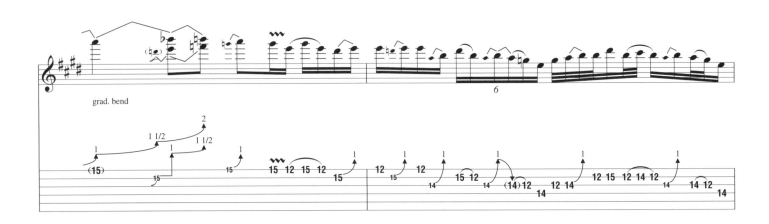

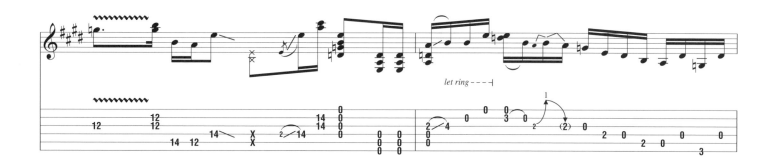

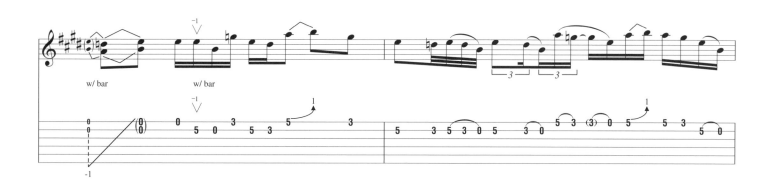

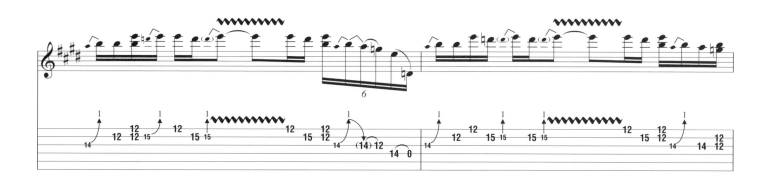

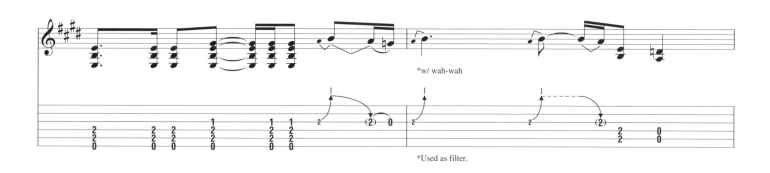

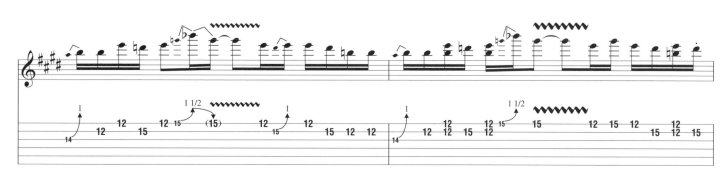

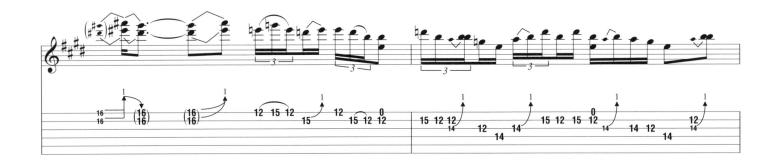

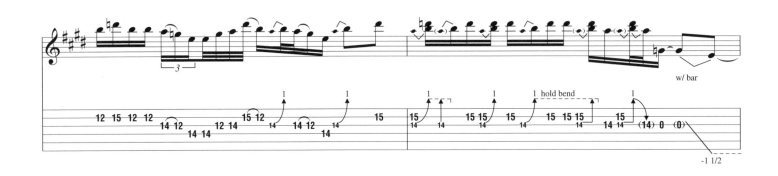

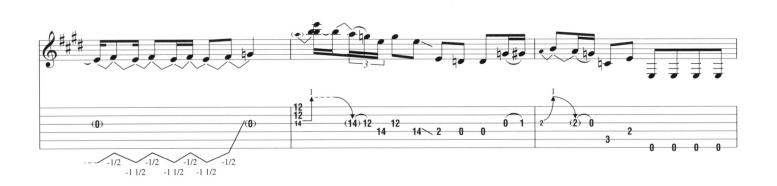

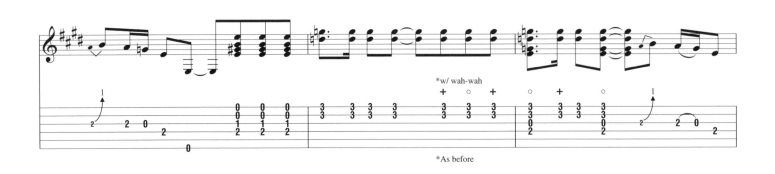

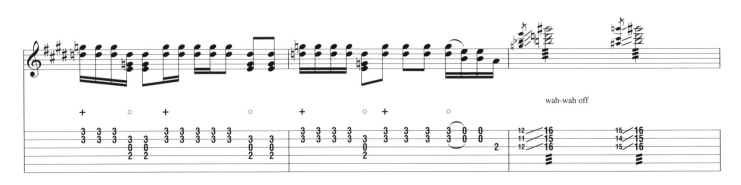

*As before

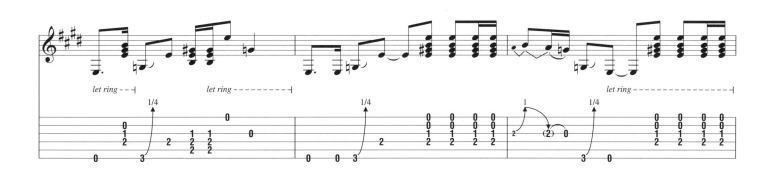

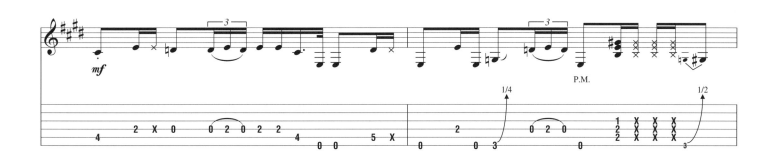

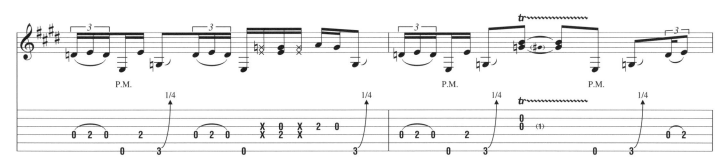

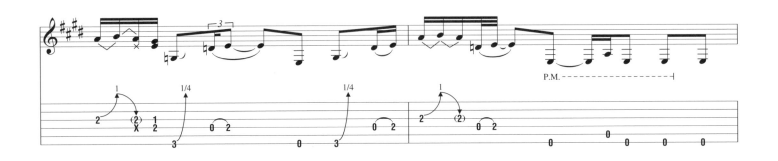

2. I did-n't

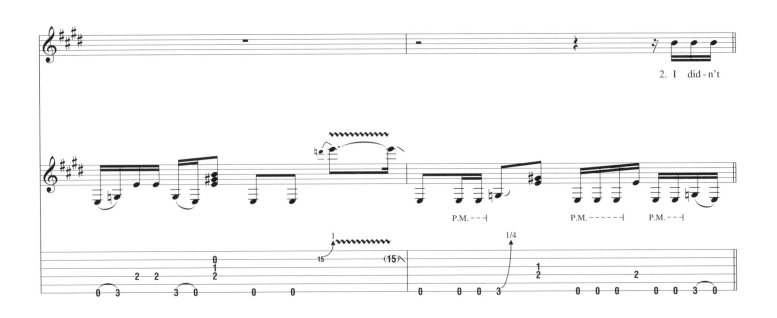

Outro-Guitar Solo

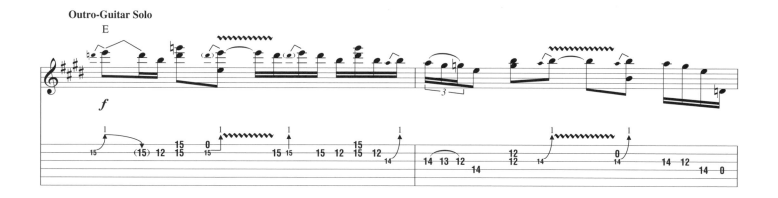

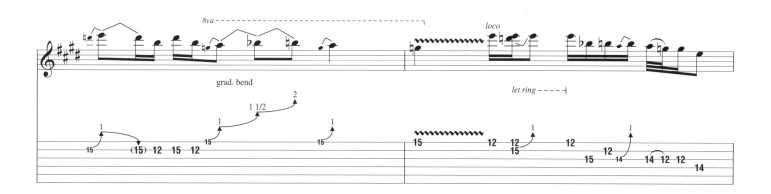

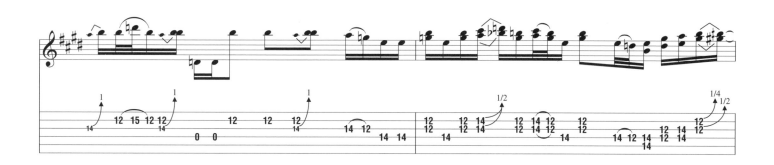

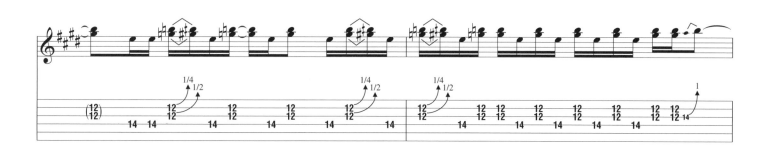

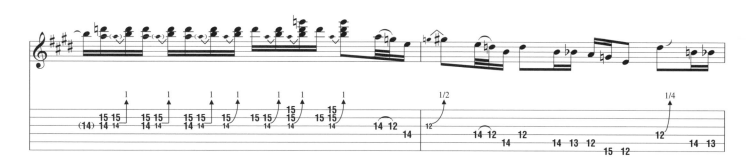

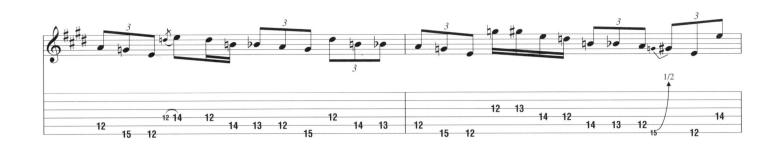

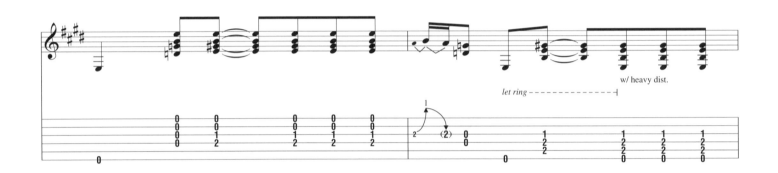

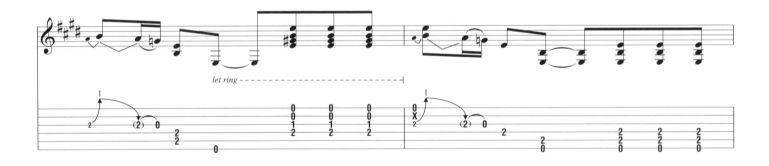

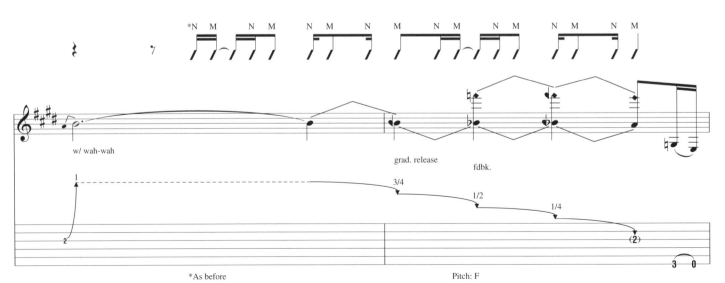

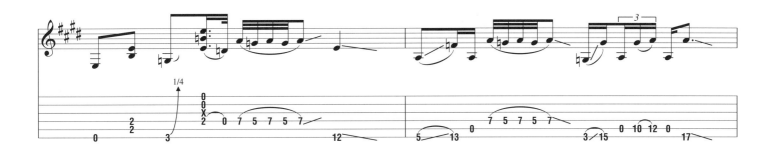

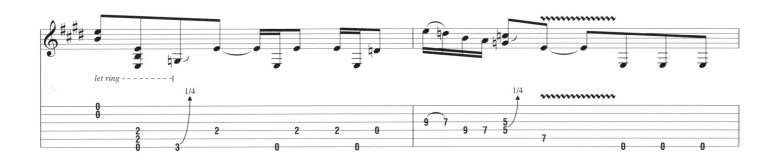

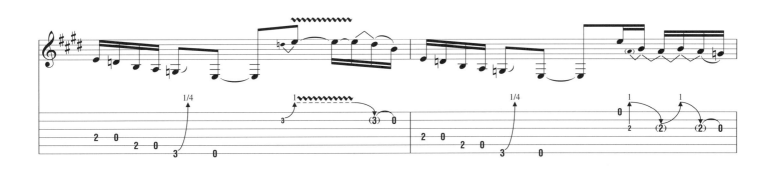

Free time

w/ fdbk. ad lib.

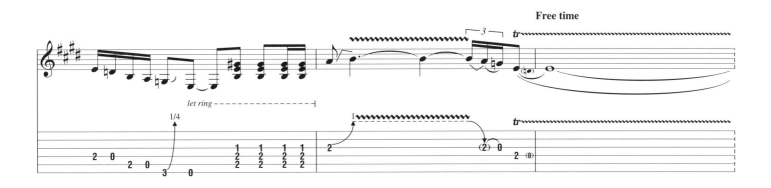

E7♯9

w/ bar

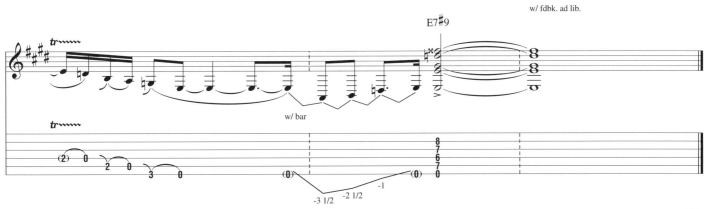

Purple Haze

Words and Music by Jimi Hendrix

Tune down 1/2 step:
(low to high) Eb-Ab-Db-Gb-Bb-Eb

10/11/68 - 2nd show

Intro
Moderately ♩ = 112

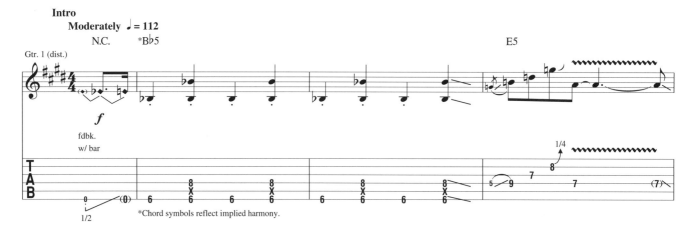

*Chord symbols reflect implied harmony.

Pitch: A
**Harm.
**Refers to 5th string only.

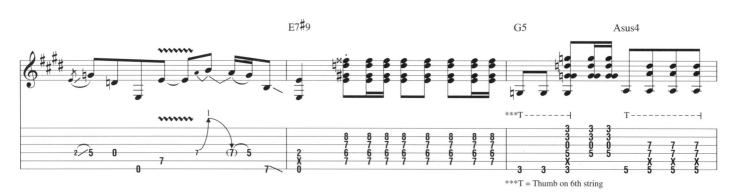

***T = Thumb on 6th string

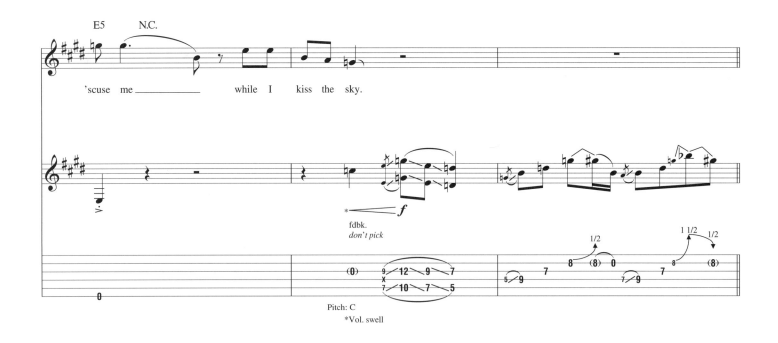

'scuse me _____ while I kiss the sky.

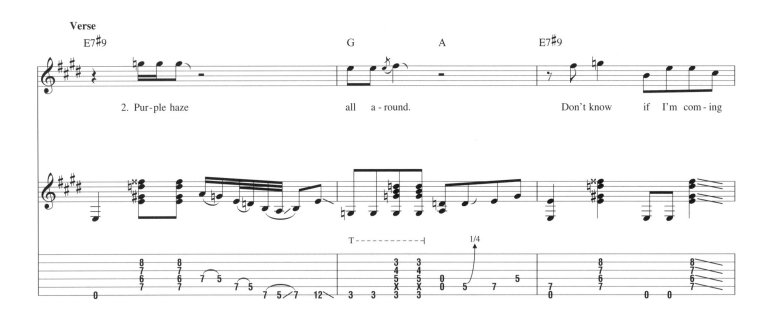

Verse

2. Pur-ple haze all a-round. Don't know if I'm com-ing

up or down. Am I hap-py or in mis-er-y? What-

ev-er it is,___ that girl___ put a spell on me.

Bridge

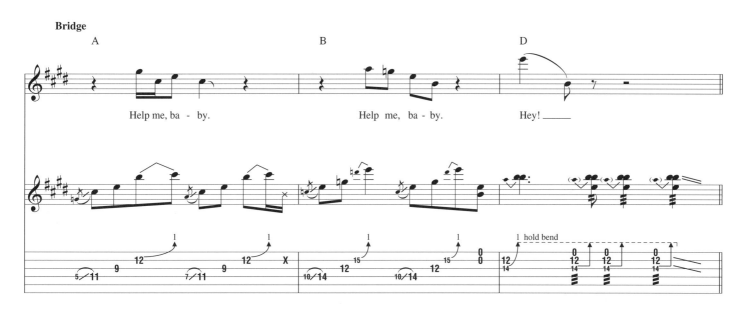

Help me, ba - by.   Help me, ba - by.   Hey! _____

Guitar Solo

*Chord symbols reflect overall harmony.

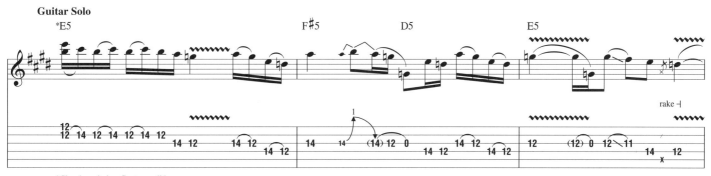

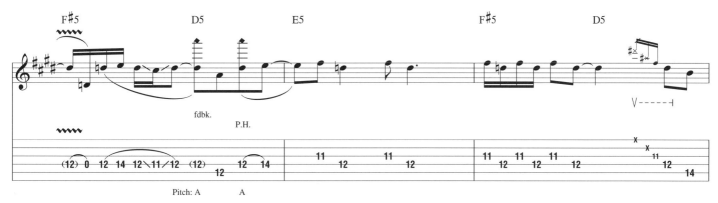

Pitch: A   A

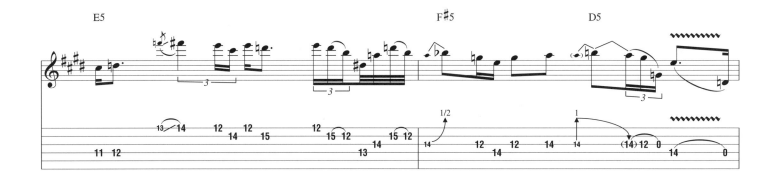

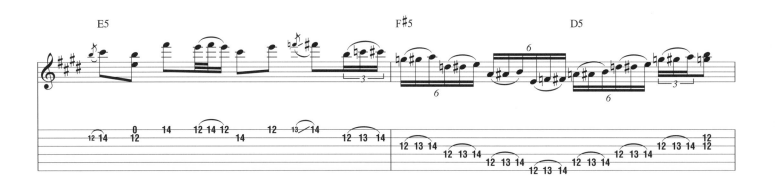

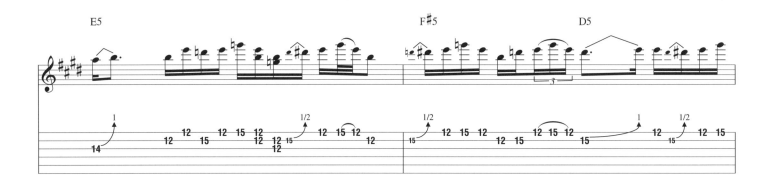

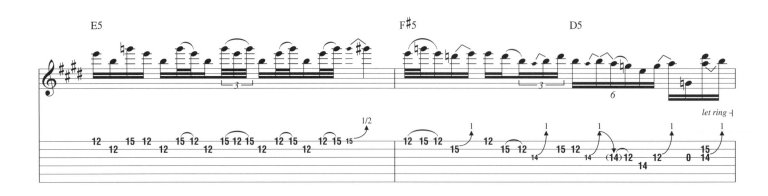

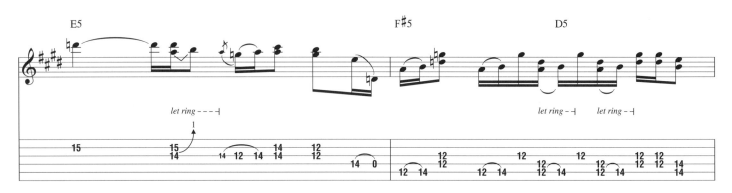

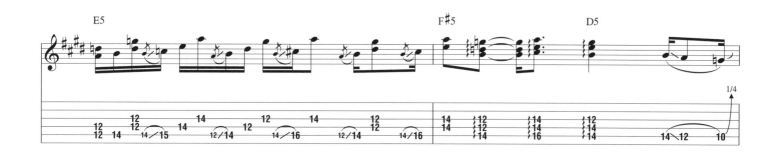

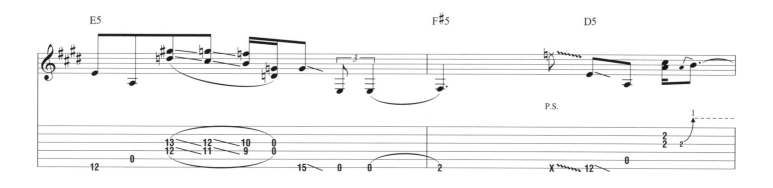

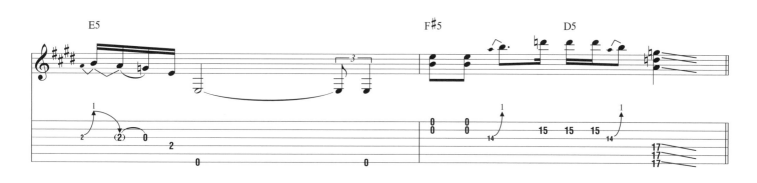

Bridge

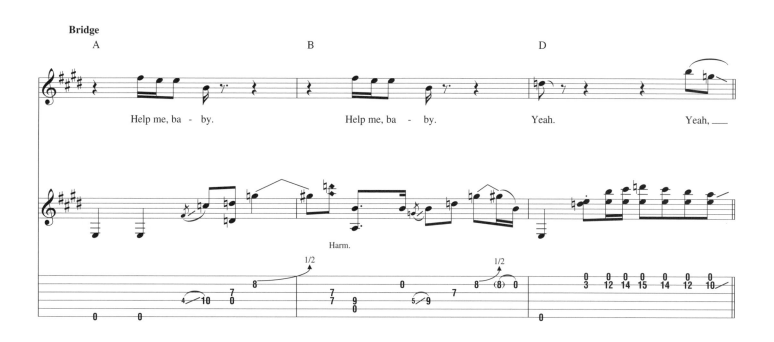

Guitar Solo

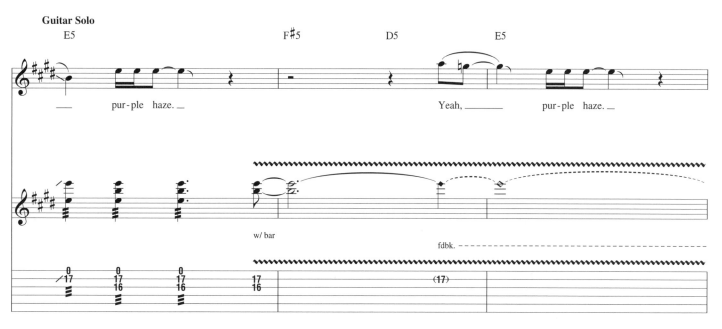

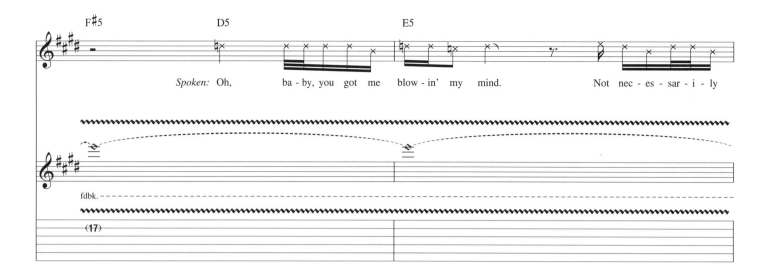

Spoken: Oh, ba - by, you got me blow - in' my mind. Not nec - es - sar - i - ly

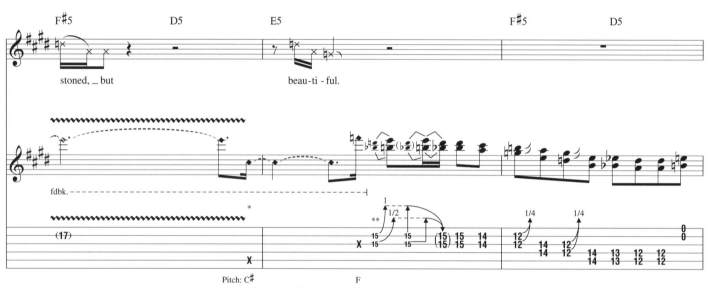

stoned, _ but beau - ti - ful.

Pitch: C♯   F

*Microphonic fdbk., not caused by string vibration.

**3rd string caught under bend finger.

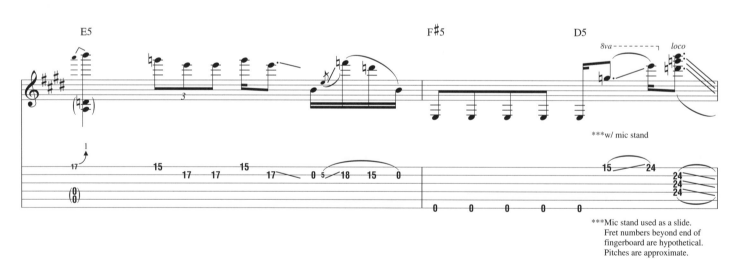

***w/ mic stand

***Mic stand used as a slide.
Fret numbers beyond end of
fingerboard are hypothetical.
Pitches are approximate.

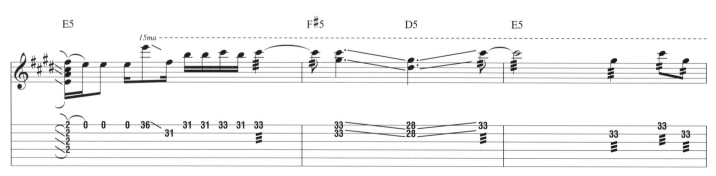

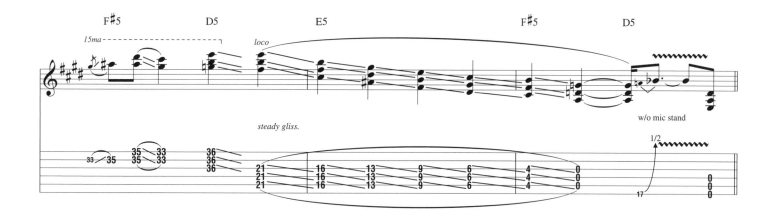

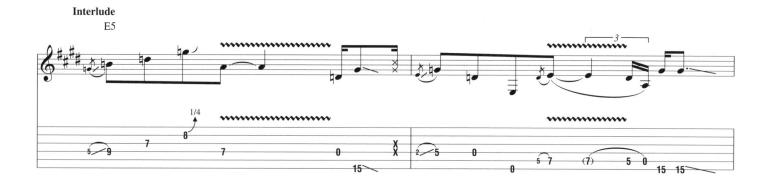

Interlude

E5

Oo!

Oo!

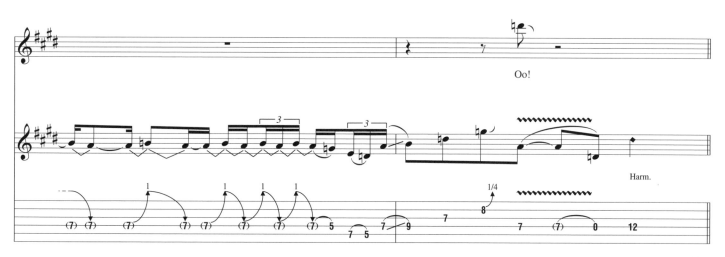

Oo!

Harm.

Outro
Free time

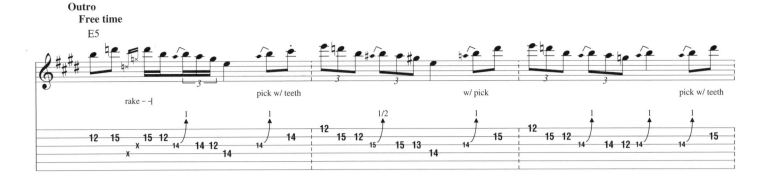

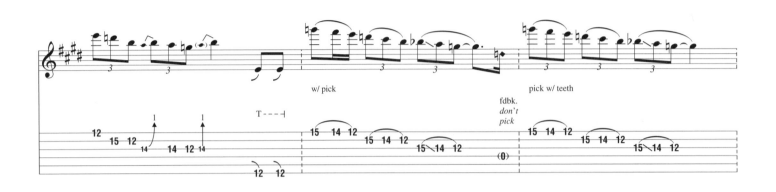

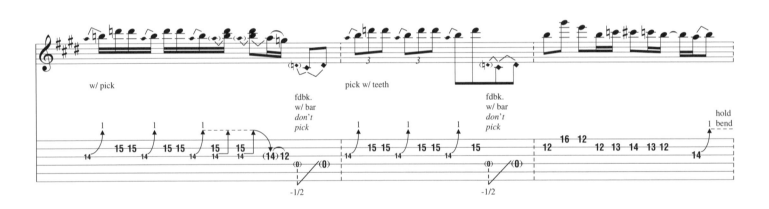

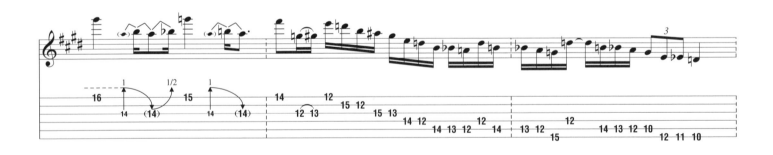

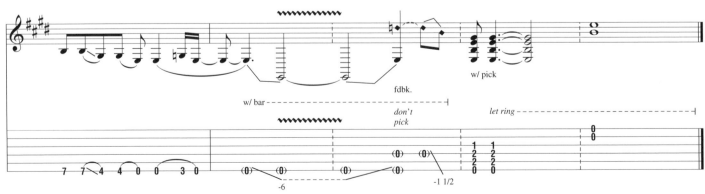

GUITAR NOTATION LEGEND

Guitar music can be notated three different ways: on a *musical staff*, in *tablature*, and in *rhythm slashes*.

RHYTHM SLASHES are written above the staff. Strum chords in the rhythm indicated. Use the chord diagrams found at the top of the first page of the transcription for the appropriate chord voicings. Round noteheads indicate single notes.

THE MUSICAL STAFF shows pitches and rhythms and is divided by bar lines into measures. Pitches are named after the first seven letters of the alphabet.

TABLATURE graphically represents the guitar fingerboard. Each horizontal line represents a string, and each number represents a fret.

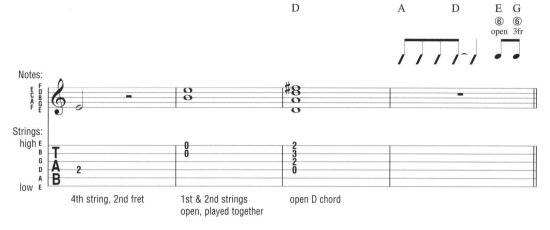

4th string, 2nd fret   1st & 2nd strings open, played together   open D chord

Definitions for Special Guitar Notation

HALF-STEP BEND: Strike the note and bend up 1/2 step.

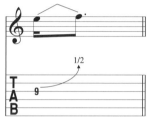

WHOLE-STEP BEND: Strike the note and bend up one step.

GRACE NOTE BEND: Strike the note and immediately bend up as indicated.

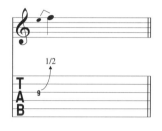

SLIGHT (MICROTONE) BEND: Strike the note and bend up 1/4 step.

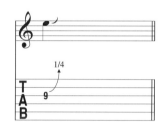

BEND AND RELEASE: Strike the note and bend up as indicated, then release back to the original note. Only the first note is struck.

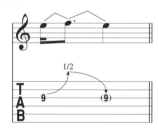

PRE-BEND: Bend the note as indicated, then strike it.

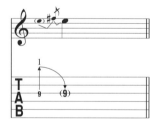

PRE-BEND AND RELEASE: Bend the note as indicated. Strike it and release the bend back to the original note.

UNISON BEND: Strike the two notes simultaneously and bend the lower note up to the pitch of the higher.

VIBRATO: The string is vibrated by rapidly bending and releasing the note with the fretting hand.

WIDE VIBRATO: The pitch is varied to a greater degree by vibrating with the fretting hand.

HAMMER-ON: Strike the first (lower) note with one finger, then sound the higher note (on the same string) with another finger by fretting it without picking.

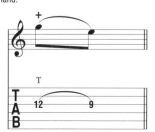

PULL-OFF: Place both fingers on the notes to be sounded. Strike the first note and without picking, pull the finger off to sound the second (lower) note.

LEGATO SLIDE: Strike the first note and then slide the same fret-hand finger up or down to the second note. The second note is not struck.

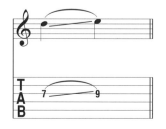

SHIFT SLIDE: Same as legato slide, except the second note is struck.

TRILL: Very rapidly alternate between the notes indicated by continuously hammering on and pulling off.

TAPPING: Hammer ("tap") the fret indicated with the pick-hand index or middle finger and pull off to the note fretted by the fret hand.

NATURAL HARMONIC: Strike the note while the fret-hand lightly touches the string directly over the fret indicated.

PINCH HARMONIC: The note is fretted normally and a harmonic is produced by adding the edge of the thumb or the tip of the index finger of the pick hand to the normal pick attack.

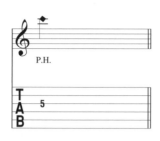

HARP HARMONIC: The note is fretted normally and a harmonic is produced by gently resting the pick hand's index finger directly above the indicated fret (in parentheses) while the pick hand's thumb or pick assists by plucking the appropriate string.

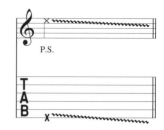

PICK SCRAPE: The edge of the pick is rubbed down (or up) the string, producing a scratchy sound.

MUFFLED STRINGS: A percussive sound is produced by laying the fret hand across the string(s) without depressing, and striking them with the pick hand.

PALM MUTING: The note is partially muted by the pick hand lightly touching the string(s) just before the bridge.

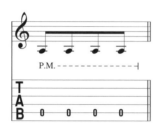

RAKE: Drag the pick across the strings indicated with a single motion.

TREMOLO PICKING: The note is picked as rapidly and continuously as possible.

ARPEGGIATE: Play the notes of the chord indicated by quickly rolling them from bottom to top.

VIBRATO BAR DIVE AND RETURN: The pitch of the note or chord is dropped a specified number of steps (in rhythm), then returned to the original pitch.

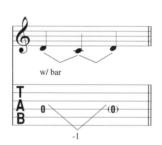

VIBRATO BAR SCOOP: Depress the bar just before striking the note, then quickly release the bar.

VIBRATO BAR DIP: Strike the note and then immediately drop a specified number of steps, then release back to the original pitch.

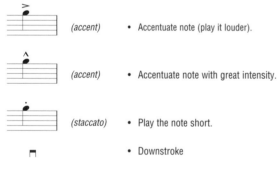

Additional Musical Definitions

(accent)	• Accentuate note (play it louder).	

∧ (accent)	• Accentuate note with great intensity.
• (staccato)	• Play the note short.
⊓	• Downstroke
∨	• Upstroke

D.S. al Coda • Go back to the sign (𝄋), then play until the measure marked "*To Coda*," then skip to the section labelled "**Coda**."

D.C. al Fine • Go back to the beginning of the song and play until the measure marked "*Fine*" (end).

Rhy. Fig. • Label used to recall a recurring accompaniment pattern (usually chordal).

Riff • Label used to recall composed, melodic lines (usually single notes) which recur.

Fill • Label used to identify a brief melodic figure which is to be inserted into the arrangement.

Rhy. Fill • A chordal version of a Fill.

tacet • Instrument is silent (drops out).

• Repeat measures between signs.

• When a repeated section has different endings, play the first ending only the first time and the second ending only the second time.

NOTE: Tablature numbers in parentheses mean:
    1. The note is being sustained over a system (note in standard notation is tied), or
    2. The note is sustained, but a new articulation (such as a hammer-on, pull-off, slide or vibrato) begins, or
    3. The note is a barely audible "ghost" note (note in standard notation is also in parentheses).

Hendrix Publications from Hal Leonard

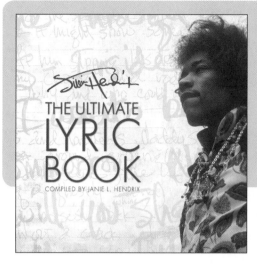

Jimi Hendrix THE ULTIMATE LYRIC BOOK
compiled by Janie L. Hendrix • Backbeat Books

Here are all of the words to the Hendrix classics you've rocked along to for years, as well as unpublished songs from "Valley of Neptune" and other hitherto undiscovered sources, gathered together. The book includes numerous examples of Jimi's handwritten lyrics, often scribbled on hotel stationary, as well as photos of Jimi to accompany every song.

00333049 Hardcover Book..$40.00

Are You Experienced
11 songs: Are You Experienced • Foxey Lady • Hey Joe • Manic Depression • Purple Haze • The Wind Cries Mary • and more.

00692930 Guitar Recorded Versions.....................$24.95
00660097 Easy Recorded Versions $12.95
00690371 Bass Recorded Versions $17.95
00690372 Drum Recorded Versions $16.99
00672308 Transcribed Scores (17 songs) $29.95

Axis: Bold as Love
13 songs: Bold as Love • Castles Made of Sand • Little Wing • Spanish Castle Magic • and more.

00692931 Guitar Recorded Versions $22.95
00672345 Transcribed Scores $29.95

Band of Gypsys
Contains note-for-note transcriptions of: Who Knows • Machine Gun • Changes • Power to Love • Message of Love • We Gotta Live Together. Includes introduction and playing tips.

00690304 Guitar Recorded Versions $24.99
00672313 Transcribed Scores $29.95

Blue Wild Angel
All 18 songs from *Jimi Hendrix – Live at the Isle of Wright*. Includes: All Along the Watchtower • Dolly Dagger • Foxey Lady • Freedom • Machine Gun • Sgt. Pepper's Lonely Hearts Club Band • and more.

00690608 Guitar Recorded Versions $24.95

Blues
10 transcriptions of Jimi's most popular blues tunes complete with an extensive introduction and photo section: Born Under a Bad Sign • Catfish Blues • Hear My Train a Comin' • Once I Had a Woman • Red House • Voodoo Chile Blues • and more.

00694944 Guitar Recorded Versions.....................$24.95

Electric Ladyland
16 songs: All Along the Watchtower • Have You Ever Been (To Electric Ladyland) • Voodoo Child (Slight Return) • and more.

00692932 Guitar Recorded Versions $24.95

Smash Hits
Hendrix's 1969 best-of compilation of 12 songs: All Along the Watchtower • Crosstown Traffic • Fire • Foxey Lady • Hey Joe • Purple Haze • Remember • Stone Free • The Wind Cries Mary.

00690602 Guitar Recorded Versions.....................$24.99
00699723 Guitar Play-Along.............................$19.95
00699835 Drum Play-Along..............................$16.95

Valleys of Neptune
This compilation matches the highly anticipated album of 12 previously unreleased Hendrix recordings. Includes: Bleeding Heart • Fire • Lover Man • Lullaby for the Summer • Mr. Bad Luck • Red House • Stone Free • Sunshine of Your Love • Valleys of Neptune • and more.

00691033 Guitar Recorded Versions.....................$22.99

West Coast Seattle Boy: The Jimi Hendrix Anthology
Here are more than 30 tracks from the boxed set of previously unreleased studio and live recordings: Castles Made of Sand • Fire • Hear My Train a Comin' (Get My Heart Back Together) • The New Rising Sun • 1983...(A Merman I Should Turn to Be) • Purple Haze • Star Spangled Banner • The Wind Cries Mary • and more.

00691152 Guitar Recorded Versions.....................$29.99

Winterland (Highlights)
This folio transcribes every note as Hendrix played them on 11 songs from the live recordings of his performances at San Francisco's Winterland Ballroom in 1968. Includes: Are You Experienced? • Fire • Foxey Lady • Hey Joe • Little Wing • Manic Depression • Voodoo Child (Slight Return) • and more.

00691332 Guitar Recorded Versions.....................$22.99

Live at Woodstock
Relive Hendrix's Woodstock performance with these 11 songs: Red House • Star Spangled Banner • Villanova Junction • and more. Includes photos.

00690017 Guitar Recorded Versions $24.95

Experience Hendrix – Book One Beginning Guitar Method
by Michael Johnson

This step-by-step process of learning music using the songs of Jimi Hendrix teaches guitar basics, music basics, music/guitar theory, scales, chords, reading music, guidelines for practicing, tips on caring for your guitar, and much more.

00695159 Book/CD Pack....................................$14.95

Jimi Hendrix – Experience Hendrix
20 of Hendrix's best: All Along the Watchtower • Bold as Love • Castles Made of Sand • Foxey Lady • Hey Joe • Manic Depression • Purple Haze • Star Spangled Banner • The Wind Cries Mary • and more.

00672397 Transcribed Scores $29.95
00307009 Piano/Vocal/Guitar $16.95

In Deep with Jimi Hendrix
by Andy Aledort

This book breaks down and reassembles the solos, riffs, rhythm figures, harmony lines, ensemble parts, and more from over 40 of Hendrix' greatest songs.

00660335 Guitar School $19.95

Jimi Hendrix Anthology
73 songs from all of his recordings: Are You Experienced? • Freedom • Gypsy Eyes • Hear My Train a Comin' • I Don't Live Today • My Friend • Stepping Stone • and more. Includes photos.

00306930 Melody/Lyrics/Chords..........................$22.50

Jimi Hendrix – Signature Licks
by Andy Aledort

Performance notes, chord voicings, scale use, and unusual techniques are included for 12 songs: Foxey Lady • Hey Joe • Little Wing • Purple Haze • and more.

00696560 Book/CD Pack.....................................$24.95

Jimi Hendrix – Learn to Play the Songs from Are You Experienced
This DVD shows guitarists how to play parts of every song on this album. Songs: Purple Haze • Love or Confusion • The Wind Cries Mary • Fire • Third Stone from the Sun • Can You See Me • and more.

00320274 DVD $59.95

Prices, contents, and availability subject to change without notice.

Study the master with these transcriptions and explorations of the techniques and tunes that made Hendrix a legend.

FOR MORE INFORMATION, SEE YOUR LOCAL MUSIC DEALER, OR WRITE TO:

7777 W. BLUEMOUND RD. P.O. BOX 13819 MILWAUKEE, WI 53213

Complete song lists online at
www.halleonard.com

0912

GUITAR RECORDED VERSIONS®

Guitar Recorded Versions® are note-for-note transcriptions of guitar music taken directly off recordings
This series, one of the most popular in print today, features some of the greatest
guitar players and groups from blues and rock to country and jazz.

Guitar Recorded Versions are transcribed by the best transcribers in the business
Every book contains notes and tablature. Visit www.halleonard.com for our complete selection.

AUTHENTIC TRANSCRIPTIONS
WITH NOTES AND TABLATURE